The Ulverstone & Lancaster Railway

The Challenge of Morecambe Bay

Leslie R Gilpin

CUMBRIAN
RAILWAYS
ASSOCIATION

Other publications by the Cumbrian Railways Association

'Cumbrian Communities' Series:

     No. 1   Grange-over-Sands *(Leslie R Gilpin)* - Out of print

     No. 2   Ravenglass *(Peter van Zeller)*

     No. 3   Dalton-in-Furness (*Rock Battye)*

     No. 4   Whitehaven *(Howard Quayle)*

'Railway Histories' Series:

     The Kendal & Windermere Railway *(Dick Smith)* - Out of print

     The Furness Railway in and around Barrow *(Dr Michael Andrews)* - Out of print

     The Coniston Railway *(Dr Michael Andrews & Geoff Holme)*

     The Track of the Ironmasters *(W McGowan Gradon - edited by Peter Robinson)*

Locomotive Histories:

     The Great Survivor - the rebuilding of Furness Railway No. 20 *(Tim Owen)*

Text © 2008 Leslie R Gilpin and the Cumbrian Railways Association

Maps © Alan Johnstone and the Cumbrian Railways Association

Photographs © as credited

**Published by the Cumbrian Railways Association,
104 Durley Avenue, Pinner, Middlesex. HA5 1JH**

**The Association is Registered Charity No. 1025436
www.cumbrianrailwaysassociation.org.uk**

Secretary, Cumbrian Railways Association, 24 Carlton Gardens, Carlisle, Cumbria, CA3 7DL

Design and layout by Michael Peascod

Printed by Lambert Print & Design, Settle, North Yorkshire. BD24 9AA

ISBN 978-0-9540232-7-0

The Cumbrian Railways Association is the local railway history group for Cumbria and North Lancashire. With a membership of over 400 it is a registered charity with the aim of promoting interest in and knowledge of the railways of this area, and the part they played in its development over the last 150 years. For more information about the Association, its activities and services, please visit our website at www.cumbrianrailwaysassociation.org.uk or write to the Secretary at the above address.

Contents

Authors note -
One of the curiosities of the English language in the nineteenth century when writing place names was to add the letter 'e' at the end. Thus in many written works of the period, including Acts of Parliament, Ulverston became Ulverstone. Within this book I have attempted to use the current spelling unless it was part of the legal title of a company, hence the town is Ulverston but the railway company was the Ulverstone & Lancaster Railway.   *LG*

Front cover:
Furness Railway 0-4-0 No. 3 hauls a passenger train across the Leven viaduct en route from Carnforth to Ulverston. At this time the viaduct only carried a single track. Note the raked columns on the upstream side are only on alternate piers. These were hinged at their bases in preparation for widening the viaduct at a future date. When the viaduct was widened, these were raised to the vertical to form bearing columns for the second track.

(Painting by Robert Nixon, Author's Collection.)

North Lonsdale Crossing. Enthusiasts gather around North Lonsdale Crossing signal box after arrival of the Stephenson Locomotive Society and Manchester Locomotive Society's 'Furness Railtour' on 27 August 1961. Without the foresight and enthusiasm of these people, many of the photographs in this book would not exist.   (CRA Photo Library ref. M00826)

Introduction

Over the smooth sands
Of Leven's ample estuary lay
My journey, and beneath a genial sun,
With distant prospect among gleams in the sky
And clouds, and intermingling mountain tops....

Wordsworth, Prelude, Book 10

The railway from Ulverston to Carnforth has always held a fascination for me. I was born within sight of the viaduct across Ulverston Canal, and indeed the canal itself, and lived my formative years either within sound of Britannias and Black 5s making their way along the Capeshead embankment, or alongside that great embankment itself. Walks to the village station as a toddler meant different things, depending on whom I was with. With my grandfather it meant a look around the goods yard, in the 'Furness Supply' depot and a stop for a chat with the staff in the booking office; he'd been the village postman and knew everybody. With my mother it was a train ride to Ulverston, Barrow or occasionally Lancaster; tickets bought through the ticket window with the polished wooden barrier to hold back the queue of others waiting to buy. With my father a more exciting train ride would be in store, a weekly runabout ticket taking us to Blackpool, Morecambe, Lakeside for a trip on Windermere, and even to Southport. On occasions we went further afield – to Bradford, changing at Carnforth (Lucozade in the buffet) and being shunted around at Wennington. Now, tickets were bought from within the booking office with its high desks and photographs of the station in its fading Victorian glory. Why was it the menfolk bought their tickets from the 'inner sanctum' but the ladies queued outside?

The goods yard went before I had chance to really discover its secrets, and the steam trains, whistling as they passed through the cutting west of the station, soon followed. Shortly afterwards, visits to Barrow inspired a different aspect to the fascination – I was sent to the library to occupy my time whilst mother did her shopping. Here a request for 'railway books' resulted in McGowan Gradon's work on the Furness Railway – a work quickly absorbed by the curious 11-year-old. Here I came to learn, if only briefly mentioned, of the Ulverstone and Lancaster Railway, the very railway running past our house. One thing leads to another, as the saying goes, and this book is the result.

I hope that in this work I can share some of that fascination. Of the determination of various men over a period of thirty years to achieve what was seen as impossible – a railway across Morecambe Bay. The impact it had on the peoples of North Lancashire and the seaward end of Westmorland as the gentle, green shores of the bay were replaced by a great, monumental, white snake as the railway embankments wound their way across the great estuaries of Leven and Kent. Suddenly, overnight, the passage of coaches, pedestrians, cattle and horses across the sands from Lancaster to Ulverston stopped, replaced by the iron horse.

Despite 150 years of change, the spirit of Wordsworth's recollection holds true, if you only care to look.

Leslie R Gilpin
Cardiff
November 2008

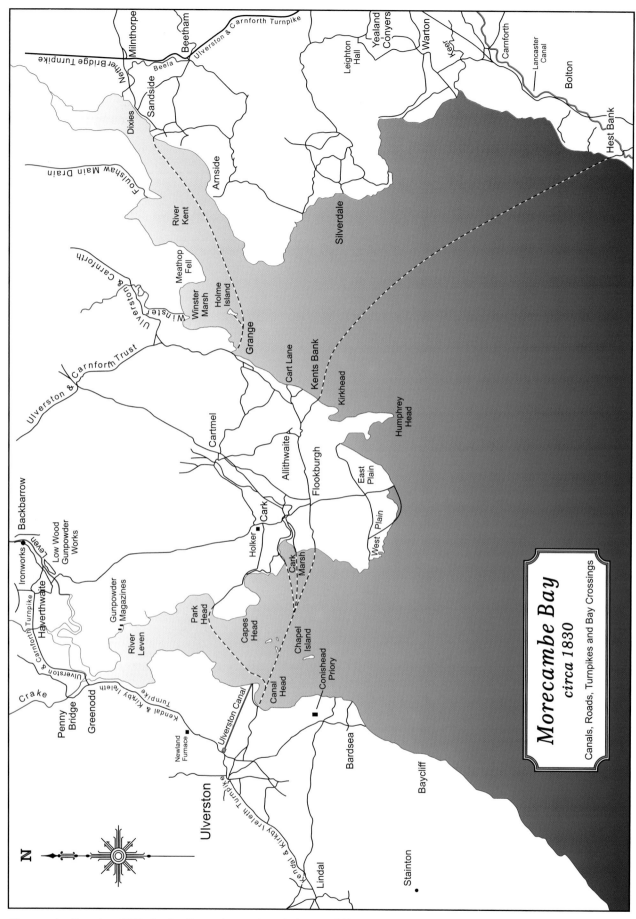

Morecambe Bay circa 1830 *showing the roads, canals and wharves of Morecambe Bay before the railway came.*

(Drawing by Alan Johnstone)

The Challenge of the Bay

1

MAN HAS BEEN living on the shores of Morecambe Bay since ancient times. Its relative isolation has been both a benefit and a hindrance to the area over the centuries. This isolation led to the development of religious establishments in the 'Dark Ages', when monastic settlements appeared at Heversham, south of Kendal, and, it is now postulated, at Urswick on the Furness peninsular. Other churches may have appeared in Cartmel, Pennington and other places around the bay, not necessarily central to a settlement but serving a wide community of farmsteads. Norsemen, forced from their outposts in Ireland by their kinsmen for trying to break away from their Scandinavian overlords, settled here. They mingled with the native Britons and the Angles who had migrated across the mainland to the area, today's towns and villages being founded by these migrants. The isolation was such that, though the area surrounding Morecambe Bay was on the edge of several kingdoms, it was perhaps largely ignored.

Following the Norman conquest of 1066, the new rulers slowly but surely consolidated their hold on the area. One means of consolidation was to establish a military base, as at Lancaster. Another involved establishing a monastic settlement, as part of bringing the culture and religion of their homeland to the whole of England, and thus was created the great Abbey of Furness and the Priories of Cartmel, Conishead and Lancaster. Certainly the monks at Furness Abbey and Conishead Priory, and possibly those at Cartmel, took advantage of one of the area's most valuable resources - iron. Not any iron ore but the best - haematite. The monks were probably the most influential people in the area from the 12th century until the Dissolution in the 1530s. They were great farmers and traders. Furness Abbey owned extensive sheep pastures and flocks across northern England, vying with their brothers at Fountains to be the greatest abbey in the north. Grain was also traded, the castle at Piel being a defensive store for grain and other goods shipped by the monks of Furness from their properties in Ireland. Cartmel too had its Irish properties but appears not to have needed defences at its wharves at Grange and Frith. The fisheries of the Leven estuary were also developed - and contested - by the monks of Cartmel and Conishead. Access by sea was a great boon at a time of poor roads.

These monastic traders also set up markets where their tenants and serfs could buy and sell. The other Lords of the adjacent manors in Furness and South Westmorland did likewise. The markets around Morecambe Bay were often accompanied by planned towns. Dalton served as the major market and administrative centre for Furness, with a smaller market at Ulverston. Cartmel had rights for markets at both the Priory - Cartmel Churchtown, as it was known - and at the town they planned and built at Flookburgh. Whilst Cartmel Churchtown may have been central to the Cartmel peninsular, Flookburgh was built astride the great highway to Furness - the Oversands road. It thus served as a place of rest on the trek from Lancaster to Furness where travellers could spend the night before or after crossing the Keer and Kent estuaries on the eastern side of the bay or the Leven on the western side, waiting for the tides to ebb. Flookburgh had burgage rights - the tradesmen who were settled there had privileges and liberties beyond that of the average Englishman. There was also the larger market at Kendal, with its flourishing woollen industry. There were markets at Milnthorpe (the port for Kendal) and Burton (both on the border of Westmorland with Lancashire and each on a highway from Lancaster to Kendal), and a market at the regional centre at Lancaster.

The Oversands road was probably the best in the area, certainly since Roman times when some metalled roads may have been built in the Furness and Cartmel areas. The main Roman and subsequent highways were further east passing through Lancaster and Kendal. When the tide is out, Morecambe Bay presents a great expanse of sand, most of which is firm and passable both on foot, by man, horse and beast, and by wheeled vehicles. The great rivers flowing into the bay are fordable at low tide. The dangers, easily overlooked by the stranger and taken for granted by the locals, are quicksands and the speed of the tide. However, given the rudimentary state of the roads elsewhere, these dangers were then a risk worth taking.

The route followed, starting from Lancaster, was to proceed over the Lune and down to the bay at Hest Bank. The traveller then headed north, passing over the estuary of the Keer before heading northwest, fording the Kent, and onto terra firma at Kents Bank or Cart Lane, west of Grange. Another route, for travellers from Yorkshire and possibly Kendal, was to cross the Kent below Milnthorpe, go past the headland at Meathop, and then over the estuary of the Winster to Grange. From Grange, Cart Lane and Kents Bank the traveller could head inland to Cartmel Churchtown and its priory, or west to Flookburgh. From Flookburgh the traveller had a choice of routes, depending on his inclination or destination. If headed for Furness Abbey, Dalton,

Crossing Morecambe Bay.
The coach, accompanied by other travellers on horseback or foot, reaches landfall while the Guide looks on. The coach service between Carnforth and Ulverstone ceased on the opening of the railway to passengers. (Author's Collection)

Conishead Priory or Ulverston, the route was due west and over the Leven estuary to Conishead, Sandside, or Bardsea, all south of Ulverston. If a shorter crossing of the sands was desired, or if travelling from Cartmel to Furness, the road was more northerly, skirting the edge of the bay, across what would later become Holker Park, to Park Head, or Frith, where Cartmel Priory had its wharf and Fishery. Here the crossing of the Leven estuary to Plumpton was shorter. From Plumpton the route was either inland over the marshes to Ulverston, or along the edge of the sands to Sandside, Conishead and Bardsea. To cater for the traveller, the monks of Furness built a hostel at Kents Bank, the monks of Cartmel built Flookburgh (as mentioned above) with a chapel, whilst the monks of Conishead built a chapel on the island of Harlside (now known as Chapel Island) in the middle of the Leven estuary. The relief of the soul was just as important as the relief of the body! At some time, certainly before the Dissolution, the monks of Cartmel and Conishead had set up other help for the traveller across the sands: guides, based at Sandside (Ulverston) for the Leven estuary and at Cart Lane (Grange) for the Kent.

For the seaman, the only harbour little affected by the tide was at Piel at the tip of the Furness peninsula. As already mentioned, Kendal had its wharf below Milnthorpe at the mouth of the Bela at what became known as Dixies and is now called Sandside, while Cartmel's were at Grange, Wyke and Frith. Otherwise any point where the shore of the bay could be accessed could be served by boat. Ulverston's harbour was the mouth of Carter Pool and the foreshore from Conishead north to Plumpton. Furness ore was shipped from various points along the eastern coast of Furness, as far north as Plumpton, whilst finished iron from the bloomeries and later ironworks were shipped from Penny Bridge, Haverthwaite and Sandside (Milnthorpe).

In later days, charcoal was shipped in the opposite direction from coastal woodlands, as demands exceeded what could be obtained from the forests close to the ironworks. The 'coal house' at Park Head still stands as a reminder of this traffic.

In some respects the tides were both a help and a hindrance. The receding tides could leave the vessels high and dry for eight or nine hours, which was time enough to load or unload onto the beach, obviating the need for a pier, before floating off on the next tide. Many vessels using the bay had flat bottoms to allow them to be beached. The restricted time when the bay was navigable was of course a limiting factor. Whilst shipping in and out of the bay and to Lancaster could follow the river channels, cross-bay traffic would have to face the shifting sandbanks. Even Lancaster suffered from the tides, although being situated several miles up the Lune from the sea. Until the eighteenth century vessels were small enough to reach Penny Bridge and Haverthwaite on the Leven, whilst on the Kent, Milnthorpe, including the area at the mouth of the River Bela and Sandside, was the port for Kendal. Penny Bridge was cut off when the Ulverston & Carnforth Turnpike was built in 1818-20 and bridged the Crake on entering Greenodd. Greenodd then developed as the main northern harbour on the Leven.

Inland, travel was more difficult, certainly until the 19th century. Although roads existed, these were little more than narrow lanes or trackways in most of the area surrounding Morecambe Bay. Wheeled vehicles were restricted to small carts, described by the 17th-century traveller Celia Fiennes as 'like little wheelbarrows'. In such circumstances pack horses were able to hold their own, and in the 18th century Kendal was the centre of a network of pack horse routes, including ones serving Ulverston and Cartmel. The main road from Kendal to Ulverston skirted the marshes and mosses

England's green and pleasant land: *this bucolic scene dates from the late 18th century, when Flookburgh was the place of rest for weary cross-bay travellers. The chapel is the second on the site, having replaced the original mediaeval building in 1777-8 and providing larger accommodation. It was located where the road from Cartmel met the over-sands road. The villages served continued to grow (Cark and Holker as well as Flookburgh itself), and this led to the chapel being extended eastwards in 1836 and having a second gallery added. It was replaced in 1900 by the large church on Station Road. The weekly market would have been held in the street behind the artist, whilst the twice-yearly fairs were held in a field behind the village close to where the station came to be built.*

(Courtesy P Taylor)

Grange from Holme Island. *When this sketch of Grange was drawn circa 1840, the place was used as a resort by a few visitors who would rent cottages for the summer months. As can be seen, the village skirted the shoreline.*
(Author's Collection)

above the tidal limits of the rivers flowing into the bay, passing via Crosthwaite, Bowland Bridge, Finsthwaite and Bouth. A more southerly route to Cartmel crossed the mosses between Beanthwaite Green (modern Levens) and Witherslack on an embankment before heading over high ground to reach High Newton and head down to Cartmel.

After 1540 and the removal of the monastic focus of trade in Furness and Cartmel, some changes affected transport in the area. The market at Ulverston soon overtook that at Dalton in importance, and it became the centre for local trade. As a consequence, cross-bay traffic headed for Sandside bound for Ulverston, rather than the more southerly road to Dalton. With the Crown taking over monastic property, they were obliged to take over the provision of guides over the Kent and Leven sands, an obligation that continues today. Over in Cartmel, 'Churchtown' (modern Cartmel village) remained as the centre for local government. It is possible that, without monastic patronage, the market at Flookburgh reduced in importance, whilst that at Churchtown flourished on a smaller scale. Otherwise little appears to have changed until industrialisation started to make its mark at the start of the 18th century.

The most significant impact in terms of industrialisation was the setting up of blast furnaces from the late 17th century in High Furness. These works exploited the ready availability of local haematite as well as charcoal and water. Restrictions on the availability of previously cheap Swedish iron together with increasing trade overseas had led to a growth in iron production around the country. Furness iron was in demand both in the local furnaces and elsewhere, especially in South Wales and Staffordshire where it was used to supplement the poorer quality local ores. The ideal mode of transporting the ore was by sea (after being carted to the shore in the small local carts). Since iron production was seen as a seasonal occupation in Furness, using agricultural labour when available, it was necessary to stockpile the ore at the point of shipment, thus enabling demand to be met around the year. Ore floors were used for this purpose and appeared at Baycliff, Bardsea and Conishead as well as further south at a hamlet called Barrow. The Furness ironworks had convenient wharves, including those at Haverthwaite, for the Backbarrow and Nibthwaite works, and at Penny Bridge. Duddon Furnace was on the other side of the Furness peninsula, served by ships running up the Duddon estuary. The anomaly was Newland Furnace, which could only be served by road (it was adjacent to the previously mentioned Kendal to Ulverston packhorse route). Over on the eastern side of Morecambe Bay was Leighton Furnace, whilst Halton Furnace was situated on the Lune above Lancaster, both being supplied by ship with Furness ore.

The latter half of the 18th century saw the widespread introduction of 'cotton manufactures' (factories) throughout the north of England, especially following the expiry of Arkwright's patents on spinning machinery. Cotton mills appeared both in isolated rural locations and in towns. One of the first significant mills was set up in 1784 on the site of a forge at Cark.

Cark owed its origins to Cartmel Priory, being the site of one of its corn mills. Following the Dissolution it had developed as a small industrial community. Apart from the ancient corn mill, which did not finally close until around 1970, the village was also home to one of the earliest paper mills in England, operating from before 1617 until around 1840, by which time it had become too small and its production methods outdated. A further industrial site was centred around a mediaeval fulling mill which, for a time, was also turned over to paper making before becoming a forge. Various suggestions have been made as to why papermaking should occur in such an isolated place as Cark, when, certainly in the early 17th century, most other paper mills were in the south-east of England. These range from the romantic (paper from which Catholic missals could be made by the recusant Prestons of Holker Hall), to the mundane (brown paper for use by the Cartmel and Kendal woolen industries). The development of a forge at Cark followed the arrival of one James Stockdale to the village. Stockdale originated from either Kellett or Bolton-le-Sands, and had been apprenticed to one of the leading merchants of Lancaster. From this he built up his own business, with estates in the West Indies and Virginia, his own shipyard (whose site was to be cut through by the U&LR at Cark), iron mines in Furness and business relationships with some of the leading industrialists of the later 18th century. As well as building a house for himself at Cark, he also persuaded a group of investors to set up the forge, whose customers included James Watt. By 1780 Stockdale's attention had been taken by that other great industry, cotton spinning, especially since Richard Arkwright's patent on the 'water frame' was due to expire. With three partners, he built a cotton spinning mill, and not just any mill. It was, for its time, a big mill, and required a massive transformation of Cark, including the draining of a mill pond, diverting the river to a lower course, and the building of the mill, associated outbuildings and five rows of workers houses. The river through the village proved insufficient to supply all the water needed to power the mill, especially in summer. Stockdale went to his friends Boulton, Watt and Wilkinson for a steam engine to allow water used by the mill to be recycled. The engine was a notable arrival and the village inn changed its name to 'The Engine'. Two further steam engines appeared at Cark, one unsuccessful but the other significant in that it infringed Boulton & Watt patents. Being a friend, Stockdale was treated lightly by the litigious engineers. The report of its detection by Boulton and Watt's spy makes amusing reading.

Supplies came by sea to a wharf at the mouth of Cark Beck (or River Eea). The demand for coal at the mill together with the increasing preference for coal over peat for domestic use meant a coal yard was set up at the village wharf.

This cotton mill, although large for its time, soon became too small, especially when the shareholding passed from Stockdale's partners to business colleagues in Lancaster. The Lancaster men owned much larger mills in the Lune Valley, capable of expansion and with a much more reliable water supply. The Cark mill was totally enclosed and incapable of growth. It was closed in the early 19th century with the engines disposed of. Sold in 1815 and converted into a corn mill, it survived in that role until it was devastated by fire in 1935.

Further north, adjacent to the Backbarrow Furnace stood another cotton works, which was to become notorious in the 1830s for its handling of (or rather disposing of) child labour. Its wharf was at Haverthwaite. A further works appeared near Penny Bridge, about a mile above that wharf. A number of cotton mills were erected in and adjacent to Ulverston, served initially by the wharves on the bay. Meanwhile at Kendal, wool remained the staple trade, with wool spinning a major industry.

The end of the 18th century saw the introduction of gunpowder manufacture. Initially, it established itself to the south of Kendal, but a further works appeared at Low Wood (on a redundant ironworks site) near Haverthwaite. Initially it imported its sulphur and saltpetre and exported its products via the Haverthwaite wharves, although these were later superseded by wharves further south on the east side of the Leven estuary. The 'Kendal' gunpowder factories were served by sea at Milnthorpe, with the turnpikes providing a good road to the works. From 1819 they were also served by the Lancaster canal.

With industrialisation came the need to improve the roads in the area. Kendal was, after all, quite a distance from its wharf at Milnthorpe. Turnpike Trusts were the obvious solution for improving transport between these points, rather than relying on the fickle nature of the parish churchwardens who would otherwise be responsible for the upkeep of the roads. The Trusts adopted various roads leading into Kendal in the 1750s, that from Nether Bridge (on the southern edge of Kendal) to Dixies (Milnthorpe wharf, north of Sandside) and Crawthorpe, on the turnpike route from Lancaster via Burton in Kendal (itself authorized in 1751), being authorized by Parliament in 1759. Only a few years later, in 1763, the old packhorse route from Kendal to Ulverston, together with the road onward through the ore mines to the Duddon estuary (giving access to Whitehaven and West Cumberland) was adopted by the Kirkby Kendal and Kirkby Ireleth Trust. This wasn't quite what it seemed, however, since the turnpiked road was still very hilly and really only suitable for pack horses.

The investors in all the new industries were local men, and they had a need to travel in order to carry out their business. These men became wealthy through trade and their houses are still a distinctive feature around the bay. Increased trade also saw the need to improve communications by post. A mail service commenced between Lancaster and Ulverston, over-sands, in the early 1760s. However, a regular stage coach service from Lancaster to Ulverston, again over-sands, did not commence until 1781. It was not until 1819 that Ulverston received an adequate 'dry' road to the outside world with the opening of the Ulverston and Carnforth Trust's roads. This was in two sections: from Milnthorpe south towards Carnforth, where it joined a re-routed portion of the Garstang and Heron Syke Trust's road (then the main road from Lancaster to Kendal) and from the Nether Bridge Trust's road at Levens Bridge,

west over the mosses and marshes to Lindale and on to Greenodd, where it joined the existing, and presumably much upgraded, Kirkby Kendal and Kirkby Ireleth Trust road.

The final developments in the early transport network in and around Morecambe Bay were canals. Until the end of the 18th century, Ulverston was separated from the bay by a mile-wide strip of marshland extending south from near Greenodd to Conishead. This had to be crossed in order to get goods to and from the wharves. The townsfolk of Ulverston decided to overcome the difficulties of carting their goods to and from the shores of the bay. In 1793 a canal was authorized from Hammerside Hill, near the point where the cross-bay road met land, for a mile and a half inland, over the marshes to a point below Hoad Hill, alongside the turnpike. Thus, from 18 November 1796, ships could be brought right to the edge of town.

Meanwhile the townsmen of Kendal had seen the middle section of the Lancaster Canal, from Preston into Lancaster, open in 1797. This brought cheap Wigan coal to the heart of Lancaster, whilst Kendal had to rely on it being shipped by sea to Milnthorpe and then carted, at a price, into their town. It was to be 1819 before the Lancaster Canal proprietors saw fit to extend their navigation over the Lune and then parallel to the main turnpike north to Kendal. Thus bulk goods could be shipped almost to the heart of the town. However, there was a drawback. Given the Lancaster Canal only ran south as far as Preston, where a tramway provided connection to a southern section (later operated as a key section of the Leeds & Liverpool Canal), vessels still used the sea route to serve Kendal. Thus Milnthorpe did not die straight away as a port, but its days were now numbered. The growth of trade in and out of Kendal led to an enterprising Hest Bank firm to erect a pier there in 1820. The Lancaster Canal passed close to Morecambe Bay at this point, and thus the firm could transfer goods from seagoing vessel to barge via a short cart road. This lasted for eleven years. In 1825 the Lancaster Canal had opened its Glasson Dock branch, thus allowing smaller vessels direct access to Kendal from the sea. Meanwhile at Ulverston some tradesmen continued to use the wharves on the bay rather than pay tolls to use the canal.

The nineteenth century started with life continuing in North Lancashire and seaboard Westmorland pretty much as it had for the previous twenty or thirty years. However change was on the way.

Whilst much of the countryside had been enclosed over the previous centuries, any cottagers and smallholders still held the same rights to gather peat for fuel and to graze their livestock on the commons and wastes of their parish as their wealthier neighbours. With their cottage gardens and possibly their strip in the communal 'town field' it was possible to enjoy the classic bucolic lifestyle described in the novels of the period. The small farmer, however, was finding things none too easy and there was a tendency for them to sell their farms to the increasing numbers of gentlemen in the district who were building up estates. The older landed families with their already large estates were even selling land amongst themselves to consolidate their landholdings.

Whether through altruistic reasons or through pure greed, the presence of town fields and undeveloped common land, marshes and mosses was anathema to the modern methods of farming espoused by the agricultural revolutionaries in England. There were thousands of acres still unenclosed and calling out to be improved, being made into fertile arable land and brought under a logical system of ownership.

The answer to the problem was Enclosure. With the authority of an Act of Parliament, the wealthy could sponsor the survey of their parish and officially reallocate the ownership of the unenclosed land. To the gentlemen it was incidental that their poorer neighbours would lose their rights to gather fuel from the peat mosses or graze their few cattle or sheep on the open hilltops. Their aim was to drain the marshes and mosses and make them productive.

The largest wholesale enclosure in the area was that covered by the 1796 Act for Cartmel Parish. The surveys and reallocation of land was not completed until 1810. Meanwhile in Furness, the cutting of the Ulverston Canal over Ulverston Common had spurred Ulverston parish to obtain an Enclosure Act in 1799, with the land allocation completed in 1812. This led to the draining of the Ulverston and Oxenholme Commons, the land to the south and west of the town.

The larger and more innovative landowners did not stop there. Beyond the high water mark around the shores of Morecambe Bay lay thousands of acres of salt marsh and sand, some of which was only covered by the sea at the equinox and solstice tides. For the cost of building an embankment this land could be reclaimed from the sea, drained, and quickly turned into first-class arable land. Some of this had been reclaimed centuries before with short embankments to protect salt marsh usually free from tidal coverage. At first the embankments were on a small scale. In Beetham parish an embankment was built between Storth and Arnside to protect adjacent mosses in 1774. In 1781 Lord George Cavendish at Holker Hall built his Grizepool embankment to stop the tides flooding his newly acquired fields on the shore as well as protecting the southern perimeter of his deer park. In Warton parish it was much later when Richard Gillow of Leighton Hall built an embankment across the marshes to the south-east of Silverdale in 1840.

Lord George Cavendish had several entrepreneurial neighbours. One was John Wilkinson, the famous ironmaster. In 1777 Wilkinson acquired much land along the river Winster, the border between Lancashire North of the Sands and Westmorland. He drained and ploughed much of the river flood plain above his residence at Castlehead. John Wilkinson also put his name to a scheme of 1786 to reclaim much of the Lancaster and Milnthorpe sands. This was promoted by John Jenkinson of Yealand and surveyed by John Longbottom. It would have reclaimed over 38,000 acres of land, diverting the river Winster north of Meathop to Nether Levens. From here the canalised and navigable channel of the Kent would have run south to near Arnside, inland to Warton and along the coast to Bare, a canal connecting into the Lune near Lancaster. The river itself was to drain into the sea off Heysham. Whilst this came to naught, a friend of Wilkinson's, the merchant James Stockdale II of Cark, achieved some degree of success in 1807 by reclaiming a section of land from the sea near Flookburgh. Stockdale, with a neighbour, erected a sea embankment to reclaim around 400 acres of Winder Marsh to produce two model farms, East Plain and West Plain. This was outside a much earlier embankment protecting part of the marsh. Unfortunately the success was to be short lived for West Plain farm. One night in 1828, the river Leven moved its course to the east side of its estuary for the first time in a hundred years. The sea reclaimed what had been its own, breaching the embankment so thoroughly that it was never rebuilt. East Plain flourished, meanwhile until wartime necessity led to much of it being commandeered to build RAF Cark and adjacent military accommodation in 1941.

Over in Furness improvements of a different sort were underway. The industrial revolution had led to an ever increasing demand for iron, and the iron ore of Furness was among the best to be had in England. As well as its use in local furnaces, it was shipped to South Wales and the Midlands to supplement the poorer ores of those districts. In the 1840s this increasingly was being carted to Barrow for shipment. Over at Kirkby the slate quarries were being increasingly exploited as the housing stock of the area was rebuilt and thatch gave way to slate.

REASONS

Why the Town of Ulverstone

OUGHT TO SUPPORT THE

Morecambe Bay Project.

When the River Leven shall have been carried in nearly a straight course, and Embanked on both sides ; the Sand, Mud, Clay, and Gravel, at present obstructing its waters, will by the rapidity of the stream and by the use of Dredging Engines, be so completely scoured out, and the river itself so deepened, that Vessels of 500 tons may almost constantly enter the port of Ulverstone and depart there from, without any hindrance ; whereby the cost of *importing* and *exporting* every kind of goods and produce will be *greatly lessened*, and Trade and Commerce be proportionably *increased*.—The port now is, just what the port of Chester *was* before the Dee was straightened in 1732—The port will, when the Morecambe Bay project is completed, be just what the port of Chester *is* at the present time, *but with a greater depth of water.*

The Iron Mines of Furness—the Copper Mines of Coniston—the Slate Quarries of Kirkby Moor, will all be worked *to three times* their present extent.

Every Stream of Water in the country, of any power, will be used extensively in the production of Manufactures of one kind or another.

Cattle, Sheep, Butter, Eggs, Cheese, Poultry, Hides, Tallow, Coppice Wood, Timber, Bark, Charcoal, Hoops, Grain of all kinds, Peas, Beans, in fact every thing the land produces, will be within *3 hours* journey (30 miles per hour) of the Manufacturing Districts and Markets, and about 8 *hours* journey of London *by the Railway*, and nearer these places than they now are by the sea, that is when the River is carried in a straight course.—Coffee, Tea, Sugar, Soap, Groceries of all kinds,—Clothing of all kinds,—Luxuries of all kinds,—in fact commodities of all kinds the produce of Foreign and other parts, will have exactly the same additional facilities offered for their introduction into Ulverstone. *The distance from Ulverstone to Newby Bridge Windermere being only about 7 or 8 miles*

The number of Visitors to the Lake Districts will be doubled—People out of the Manufacturing Districts will purchase Land in the beautiful surrounding country and erect Residences there—Great part of the sum to be expended on the works of the Morecambe Bay project, (£434,000,) will find its way to Ulverstone.

Seventy Square miles of Country now worse than a desert, will be brought into cultivation within the immediate neighbourhood of the Town, giving employment to thousands.

Thus will the Town of Ulverstone at last become a busy and thriving place—what it has long vainly strived to be,—without possessing hitherto the means—for in fact there are more *Sellers* than *Buyers* in the place, the very reverse of a state of prosperity—in other words *Trade* is *wanting ;* but may now be had, if the inhabitants will but seize the present golden opportunity, and *make hay while the sun shines ;* if not, they must as Mr. Rastrick has well said, remain in the *back settlements for ever !*

But it is argued that a new Port will arise at Leonard's Point, by which Ulverstone will be ruined—what folly ! Where are the Seaports situate at the *Mouths* of Rivers and Estuaries in any part of Great Britain ?—There are I may say absolutely, almost none, for it would be *false* in *principle so to place any Seaport,*—accordingly they are always found as far up in the interior, as Vessels of considerable tonnage can navigate ; because as the chief part of the *Exports* are *obtained* from the *Interior*, and the chief part of the *Imports* are *consumed* in the *Interior*, there is the least amount of cost of transport incurred by having the port as near the Market (the Interior) where the Mercantile Commodities are *obtained* and *consumed* as possible ; hence it is quite clear Ulverstone cannot be superseded by Leonard's Point—Lancaster is not superseded by Glasson.—In proof of all this we have the *Ports in the Clyde* all far from the mouth of the Frith—similarly situated is *Carlisle*,—also *Lancaster*,—*Preston*,—*Liverpool*,—*Chester,*—*Bristol,*—*London,*—*Hull,*—*Stockton,*—*Newcastle,&c.&c.*——The least consideration will make it clear that all these, many of them *the very first Ports in Great Britain*, are placed *as far as possible* in the Interior, that is as far as *Vessels of Burthen can Navigate*,—To stop at the Mouth of a River to discharge a Cargo, would be no better than landing on some Island (for instance on the Isle of Man or Walney) where it must again be shipped to the place of consumption on the main land.—Who would now land Goods at Barrow were the port the best in the world ?—the cartage afterwards would eat up every thing.

Glasgow is	40 miles from the	Mouth of the Frith of Clyde	
Port Glasgow	25	do.	
Greenock	20	do.	
Carlisle	15 from the Mouth of the Solway Frith		
Lancaster	7 from Mouth of Lune	......	
Preston	14 from Mouth of Ribble	......	
Liverpool	4 from Mouth of Mersey	......	
Chester	20 from Mouth of Dee	......	
Bristol	7 from Mouth of Avon	......	
London	60 from Mouth of Thames	......	
Hull	25 from Mouth of Humber	......	
Stockton	12 from Mouth of Tees	......	
Newcastle	11 from Mouth of Tyne	......	

Not so situate by *chance* or *accident* but because the several Rivers cease to be navigable for *large Vessels precisely* at the very places where the Towns are placed.

Goods intended for *Shipment*, obtained all around Whitehaven, will be *Shipped* at *Whitehaven.*

Goods intended for *Shipment*, obtained all around Lancaster, will be *Shipped* at Lancaster.

Where then is the Country through which the Railway will pass that can supply Goods or produce, for shipment at Leonard's Point ?

STEPHEN SOULBY, PRINTER, MARKET-PLACE ULVERSTON,

A proof copy of James Stockdale's handbill, dated 22 January 1839. He personally arranged for this to encourage the townsfolk of Ulverston to support the West Cumberland, Furness and Morecambe Bay Railway.
(Courtesy Lancashire CRO, ref. DP484/5)

Railway Mania

2

Canal Locks, Ulverston

Canal Foot, Ulverston. *The lift bridge straddles the lock giving access to the canal from the sea. The canal was officially closed by the LMSR in 1946 and at some time later the outer lock gates were encased in concrete. The lift bridge was replaced by a fixed bridge around the same time.*
(Author's Collection)

IN ORDER TO understand the first phase of railway promotion around Morecambe Bay we must turn our attention to West Cumberland, which had blossomed throughout the industrial revolution as a centre for coal and iron ore mining. Its coal was shipped primarily to Ireland, with Whitehaven becoming a major port in the 19th century. At several points ironworks had sprung up to exploit the ore. The Lowthers, earls of Lonsdale, had developed Whitehaven and owned and exploited the local mineral rights, whilst further north the Curwen family developed Workington and the Senhouse family developed Maryport through having similar mineral rights and estates.

In the 1830s the tentacle of modern railways was extending north from London to Birmingham and the North-West of England. Their advantage of speed over roads and canals was proving itself for both passenger and goods traffic. The West Cumberland landowners and businessmen could see that a railway connection would be of benefit to their region, which otherwise could become isolated. This was first reflected in August 1835 when the Carlisle Journal carried an editorial reviewing the options facing the railway companies as their lines headed north, and of course favouring the option of a 'west coast' route through Carlisle to Glasgow and Edinburgh.

In the October of 1835 railways were either built or authorised from London as far as Preston. The Grand Junction Railway directors, keen to ensure that the trunk route to Scotland should be over their railway, instructed their engineer, Joseph Locke, to review the options for a railway line from Preston to Carlisle. Locke recommended a route through Lancaster, up the Lune valley, under Shap Fell and through Penrith to Carlisle.

Having heard of this scheme through acquaintances involved with the development of Fleetwood, it would appear that a young engineer, Hyde Clarke, was inspired to suggest an alternative route for the railway to Scotland. In 1836-7 he made a survey for a railway from Lancaster, via the coast to Dumfries. He also commissioned a survey from there to Glasgow. These, he later claimed, were the origins of the railway across Morecambe Bay and the spur to the formation of committees in both West Cumberland and Furness to promote such a railway.

The merchants and landowners of West Cumberland, led by Captain Sir Humphrey le Fleming Senhouse of Seascale Hall (hereafter referred to as Sir Fleming Senhouse) formed the 'Caledonian Railway Committee'. In September 1836 they attempted to get George Stephenson to produce a report for a railway from Lancaster, around the coast to Whitehaven, Workington and Maryport and on to Carlisle. Whilst he surveyed a route for the Maryport & Carlisle Railway of Fleming's cousin, Humphrey Senhouse, in October 1836, for some reason he did not oblige them with a survey further south.

In 1837, whilst the M&CR Bill was proceeding through Parliament, a further approach was made to Stephenson by the Whitehaven, Workington and Maryport Railway Committee (it was referred to under various titles between 1836 and 1839). He had already provided them with a survey for a railway between those towns in March. Now he took up the commission for an 'ocular survey' of the route south of Whitehaven.

Interest in this scheme extended to Furness, where the leading lights of Ulverston and district formed their own Railway Committee at some point in 1837. Their number included:

William Gale, Gentleman of Bardsea Hall and Lightburn, Ulverston;
Mr Dodgson;
Charles Storr Kennedy, proprietor of Furness Iron Ore Mines;
Mr Philip Hartley, Cotton Spinner, Ulverston;
Thomas Gibson;
George Hartley, Cotton Spinner, Ulverston;
R Francis Yarker, Solicitor, Ulverston and Secretary to the Ulverston Canal Navigation;
Mr W Satterthwaite, Banker, Ulverston;
Mr Denney;
Mr F Town;
Stephen Soulby, Printer, Ulverston;
Joseph Jopling, Mineral Agent for the Earl of Burlington, Furness Abbey;
Mr Crosthwaite;
Mr Salthouse;
Mr Sawrey;
Mr Postlethwaite of Broughton;
Mr James Stockdale, Gentleman of Cark;
Mr Roper of Newland, Partner in Messrs Harrison Ainslie & Co., Newland, near Ulverston;
Mr Roger Postlethwaite.

One of this band, James Stockdale III, had first-hand experience of sea embankments in Morecambe Bay after inheriting his father's West Plain farm. He drew up a cross section of a suitable embankment for the scheme. This was based on the work he had to do on the original West Plain embankments near Flookburgh in order that they could handle unusually high tides in 1819. Intriguingly, whilst his plan suggested the embankment be wide enough for a single line of railway during construction, he envisaged the final railway to be laid on the reclaimed land inside it. His plans were submitted to both the Ulverston and Whitehaven committees.

Stephenson's men began work on 1 August 1837 and by the 16th he was able to recommend a railway, his Grand Caledonian Junction Railway, from Lancaster to Whitehaven and on, over the previously surveyed route, to Maryport and Carlisle. This included carrying the railway across the Kent and Keer sands on a stone embankment from Hest Bank in an arc to Humphrey Head, across Winder Moor (within sight of Stockdale's West Plain embankment), and on across the Leven estuary on a further stone embankment via Chapel Island. It would then proceed across Furness, including cuttings and a tunnel from Pennington to Kirkby Ireleth. Here a further stone embankment would allow the line to cross the Duddon and so proceed up the Cumberland coast. Stephenson expected to reclaim 20,000 acres from Morecambe Bay, with the possibility of a further 20,000 acres. The river channels would be canalised. He expected iron mines to be opened up along the route across Furness.

Thinking at that time was that such a railway must be part of the great Trunk Route from the Capital to Scotland; and there could only be one such route. The gentlemen of West Cumberland and Furness were so enthused by Stephenson's report that they had copies printed up and circulated among friends in both areas. The Caledonian, West Cumberland and Furness Railway committee was formed. The scheme was viable and it would benefit their neighbourhoods. But there was the spectre of the inland route. Public meetings were called in Whitehaven and Ulverston in December 1837, agreeing that a Petition be raised to Parliament, calling for a Government Surveyor to review the rival routes. It fell on deaf ears.

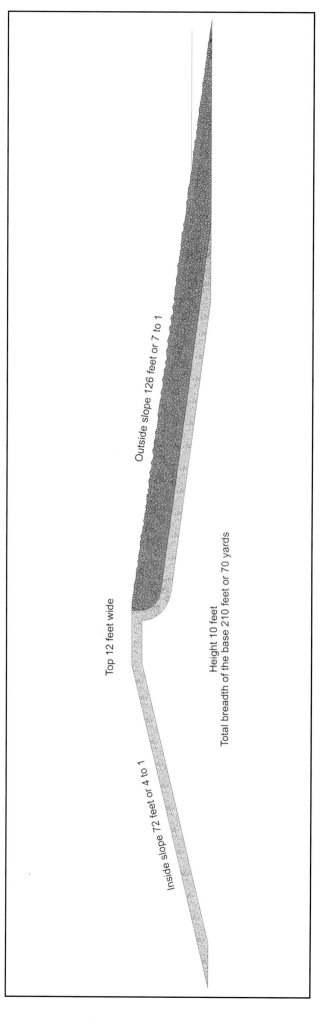

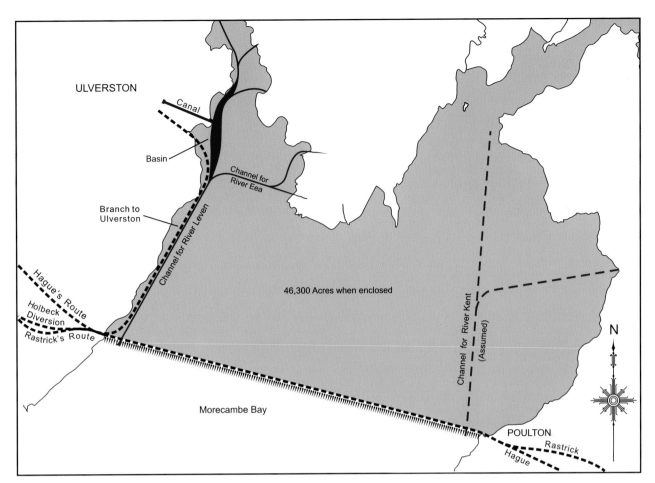

Above:
West Cumberland, Furness & Morecambe Bay Railway. *Based on John Hague's plan, this clearly shows the extent of land reclamation which attracted the West Cumberland railway committee, both to subsidise railway construction through sale of the land and through the development of the land by the speculative investors.*
(Based on a plan in the Cumbria CRO, redrawn by Alan Johnstone)

Left:
Stockdale's proposed embankment. *James Stockdale submitted this proposal for a sea embankment to the West Cumberland railway committees. It is based on local practice and is similar to those which enclosed his father's West Plain estate at Flookburgh.*
(From a drawing in the Cumbria CRO, redrawn by Alan Johnstone)

Below:
John Hague's embankment. *Hague planned to build a wooden viaduct across the bay, through which he would drop rocks to form the core of his embankment. Silting would result inland of the embankment, which itself would be covered in a casing of sand.*
(Based on a plan in the Furness Collection, Barrow-in-Furness Library Local History Collection, redrawn by Alan Johnstone)

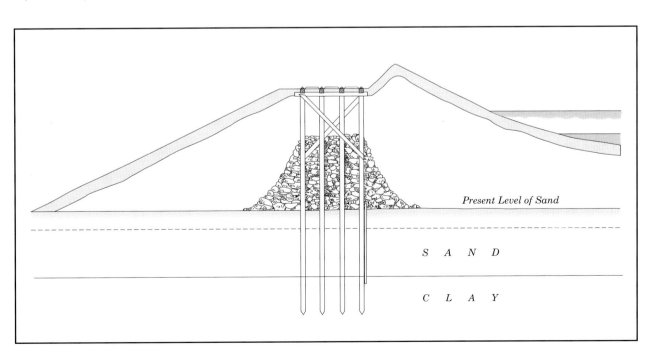

By April 1838 the Committee had raised £272 12s 0d of the £600 required to obtain 'an effective survey', largely from West Cumberland interests headed by Sir Fleming Senhouse and Henry Curwen of Workington but with Thomas Ainsworth of The Flosh, Cleator, Ironmaster, subscribing the major contribution of £50. In Furness Francis Yarker acted as agent. A staunch supporter was James Stockdale III, of Cark Yarker received 6 copies of the blank subscription list and was quickly able to find supporters, including Stockdale, to go out amongst their neighbours raising money. Stockdale even offered to double his five guinea subscription if the £600 necessary wasn't immediately raised. Both men could see the benefit of the railway, with its navigable channel to Ulverston across thousands of acres of prime agricultural land.

John Hague was engaged to provide a detailed survey for a line across Morecambe Bay and the Duddon Sands. Hague headed up to North Lancashire in May, having called upon the Earl of Burlington on the 18th of that month to gain his lordship's opinion of the scheme. Burlington, well acquainted with the bay, wasn't convinced at all.

Stockdale caught the 'railway bug' but his reasons may have been not so much because of the benefits of the railway to Ulverston but rather as to the opportunity it would give to acquire land reclaimed following the erection of Hague's embankment.

Yarker's interest was probably that of his employer, the Ulverston Canal Navigation Company. Ever since its opening in 1796, access to the Ulverston Canal was limited by the tides. Apart from being accessible only twice a day, the changing course of the River Leven often meant the entrance lock could only be reached through shallow waters at high tide or could even be silted up completely. Hague's scheme might mean canalising the rivers running into the bay, thus ensuring year-round access to the Canal via a reliable channel. Milnthorpe would similarly benefit. Also of benefit to Ulverston would be the provision of a branch railway along the river channel embankment.

In July 1838, whilst Burlington was looking around his slate quarries on Kirkby Moor, Joseph Jopling, his local agent, was voicing support for the scheme to his master. The public thought Jopling represented Burlington's opinion at the time. In fact, that was far from the truth. Burlington was beginning to lose faith in Jopling's opinion, certainly as a quarry manager! Burlington thought it a 'very wild scheme'.

Stockdale and other Lancashire investors showed a keen interest in the work of Hague and his men, frequently corresponding on their progress. One of these Lancashire investors, Edward Dawson of Aldcliffe Hall near Lancaster, had undertaken some significant reclamation in Lincolnshire. He and Stockdale regularly discussed the growing of crops on the recovered land. Hague personally wrote to Stockdale on 20 August 1838 to inform him of the completion of his survey.

Hague's plan was more ambitious than Stephenson's. He proposed a railway crossing Morecambe Bay in a dead straight line from Poulton (Morecambe) to Leonard's Point on the Furness shore. The Duddon crossing was to the south of Stephenson's. Ulverston would be served by a branch line running over the reclaimed land, off the Furness shore alongside the channel to be made for the River Leven. 46,300 acres of land would be reclaimed.

In Ulverston, Messrs Gale and Yarker were rather worried with Hague's report and plan. Whilst the plan showed a navigable channel for the Leven, the report made no such proposal. Despite knowing that there was little real benefit in it to the railway scheme, Yarker wrote to the Whitehaven Committee expressing his opinion that support from Ulverston would fall away should there be no navigable channel. Of course he would say that - he was a representative of the Ulverston Canal company! Several of the Ulverston Committee were shareholders of the Canal and their neighbours had interests in the shipping to Ulverston, Greenodd and elsewhere in the Leven estuary.

In the summer of 1838, the Committees were so confident in the scheme that they appointed London lawyers Haslam and Bischoff to act as Parliamentary agents. Bischoff became active at once, writing to advise Yarker of the information that was needed in order to proceed with an application to Parliament. More detailed plans were required than those drawn up by Hague, together with information on landowners and occupiers who would be affected by the scheme. Not only would owners of the land to be used for building the railway be affected, but those owning land adjacent to the bay and Duddon estuary inside the proposed embankments together with merchants and shipowners would also need to give their assent or otherwise.

One of the first actions was for Yarker to ask Jopling to suggest the traffic flows likely along a branch line from Ulverston. His response highlighted the importance of iron ore and slate traffics. Passengers were listed thirteenth in his list. He could not, however, supply any tonnage figures. One thing he was certain of, there would be no benefit to the railway investors in making a navigable channel to Ulverston.

In September 1838, the promoters engaged the engineer John U Rastrick to carry out their full Parliamentary survey, taking into account Hague's own report and survey. Rastrick was busy surveying the Edinburgh and Glasgow Railway at the time. Further subscriptions to defray the subsequent shortfall of £200 in the Committees' funds were called for!

That November the initial subscriptions for shares in the West Cumberland, Furness and Morecambe Bay Railway Company were being collected. However, it would appear that the sums were relatively small. The biggest subscriber was Gilfred William Hartley of Rose Hill, Whitehaven (a leading M&CR shareholder) with a deposit for forty £50 shares. James Stockdale and William Gale each paid their deposit for twenty shares. Notably absent from the lists of investors were the Earls of Lonsdale and Burlington. Supportive letters were published in the Lancaster and Preston newspapers to drum up support from North Lancashire. Public meetings were also held in Whitehaven, Ulverston and Lancaster, where John Hague demonstrated a model of his proposed embankment and its method of construction.

By this time interest was being shown from 'Scotch people'. These were Scottish railway promoters looking for a southern outlet to their proposed line from Ayrshire, through the Nith Valley and Dumfries to Carlisle. Support for the scheme was coming from the Glasgow, Kilmarnock & Ayr, Glasgow, Paisley & Greenock and Edinburgh & Glasgow railways. The railway from London had opened as far as Preston in October and there was a gap to fill. The 'Shap' route, supported by the Grand Junction Railway, was already linked to Locke's proposed line from Carlisle to Glasgow. The WCF&MBR was their only independent option.

The question of the rival routes was again worrying the promoters. In December 1838, a memorial was sent, via Burlington, to the office of the First Lord of the Treasury, requesting yet again that a Government Engineer recommend the best route for a railway from Lancaster to Carlisle. The First Lord was, of course, the Prime Minister. Again this was to be unsuccessful, it being the Government's view that this was a Parliamentary matter and not one for the Government to interfere in.

Although there had been initial enthusiasm from the townsmen of Ulverston, when it came to actual investment in the railway as a Company doubt had set in. As subscriptions for the railway proceeded, Stockdale had Yarker print a poster 'Reasons Why the Town of Ulverstone ought to support the Morecambe Bay Project'. These were posted around the town in January 1839. In it Stockdale (anonymously) highlighted reasons why Ulverston would benefit: ships of up to 500 tons could reach the port, thus reducing the costs of goods and increasing trade; the mines and quarries would expand; the produce of the town and district would be only 3 hours from the manufacturing districts by rail and closer by sea; the number of visitors would be doubled; 70 square miles of land would come into cultivation and employ thousands, and thus Ulverston would thrive! He further argued that Ulverston's distance from the sea would be no disadvantage since ports such as London, Bristol and Glasgow were all well inland, at the navigation limits of their respective rivers!

By the time Rastrick's report and plans arrived (they were forwarded from the Whitehaven secretary to Yarker on 4 January 1839), over £40,000 had been subscribed to the railway, apparently before any Prospectus had been published. At this point the company made a subtle change to its name: literally as Yarker had the proofs of the prospectus ready, its title was changed to the West Cumberland Railway and Morecambe Bay Inclosure Company! Capital to be raised was £1,500,000 in 20,000 Shares of £50 each. The deposit was £1 per Share, although £2 10s 0d was being considered. The prospectus listed the provisional committee of 10 'London' members and 22 'Country' members. The London members, chaired by John McTaggart MP, included the London architect Lewis Cubitt (who would later achieve fame as designer first of the South Eastern Railway's Bricklayers Arms station and later of Kings Cross station). The Country members were led by the Senhouse cousins, Humphrey and Fleming, and nine other West Cumberland worthies, six Furness men, including Stockdale and Gale, four from Lancaster and Preston and one Scot, James Smith, merchant and amateur inventor from Deanston, Stirlingshire. Messrs Yarker & Postlethwaite were listed alongside Haslam & Bischoff and Wilson & Perry of Whitehaven as company solicitors.

The promoters were keen to emphasise the utility of their railway and its connections across the lowlands of Scotland and also the closeness of Whitehaven, by sea, to Belfast and Northern Ireland. They were also keen to emphasise how, with the sale of reclaimed land even at reduced rates, the company could reclaim 70% of their construction costs and generate gross revenues of £100,000 per annum. In other words, investors could expect to see a handsome profit from the railway within five years.

Two key people had yet to show their colours regarding the West Cumberland Railway. One was the aged Earl of Lonsdale and the other was the Earl of Burlington. Lonsdale was one of many coal owners in West Cumberland, and perhaps he was happy to see his neighbours promote the railway and thus benefit his estates without investment from himself. Burlington's support would be more significant since his Holker estate bordered Morecambe Bay and the land to be reclaimed. On 29 January 1839 at the request of Sir Fleming Senhouse, Yarker wrote to Burlington, via his Agent, Benjamin Currey, suggesting that his Grace subscribe to the company. Burlington's response was pretty direct. Whilst he had put the petition forward to the Treasury, and been told of its rejection, he could not support the scheme, certainly without further information.

In April Yarker was writing to key supporters in the Ulverston area inviting them to obtain and promote subscriptions for the scheme. They were also invited to a meeting of the Provisional Committee at the Sun Hotel in Ulverston on 1 May to report on their progress. That month the prospectus was being circulated amongst a wider range of potential investors.

In an attempt to persuade Burlington that the scheme was feasible and worth supporting, Hague and Rastrick called on the Earl at his London home on 27 June. Whilst he was still unconvinced of the scheme, he was now seeing that something may come of it.

The provisional directors saw Stockdale as a key ally in dealing with his neighbour, the Earl of Burlington. Burlington was a major landowner in the area, with his seat at Holker Hall. The Earl was not in favour of the scheme and had to be won round. On 25 July 1839 Edward Dawson of Lancaster suggested to Stockdale that 'his Lordship's (or rather Lady Burlington's) objection arises from the idea that the view from Holker will be injured by the removal of the water'! Dawson had discussed this with Hague, McTaggart and Bischoff. The suggestion Stockdale was to put to Burlington was the 'possibility of damming up 2 or 300 acres to form a sheet of water below the house'. Burlington would listen to arguments, Dawson suggested. Meanwhile Stockdale corresponded with Dawson and others on land reclamation, considering some recent schemes in Lincolnshire.

On the 29th Yarker ended a letter to Stockdale 'I auger great success from your interview with the Earl'. It cannot have been enough for two weeks later Dawson informed Stockdale that he had met the Earl's quarry manager, Jopling, to impress upon him the benefits of a branch line to the quarries. Jopling did Dawson's bidding that August. During a visit to Kirkby Quarries the topic was discussed and Burlington stopped further work on a railway he was building on the Duddon sands at Kirkby in the event of a branch line being built from the proposed trunk line.

Following a meeting of the Ulverston Board of Guardians on 1 August 1839, Burlington met William Gale and discussed the prospects of the scheme. He came away with the impression that Gale's view was that the scheme was unlikely to be pursued. On that Sunday (the 4th) he accompanied his wife and children on a walk around his park at Holker and along the foreshore. Lady Blanche expressed her opposition to the scheme to her husband - the committee were right! He was not to meet neighbour Stockdale until 2 September. Stockdale was experimenting in the possibility of growing potatoes, grasses and other crops in the sands of Morecambe Bay and Burlington went with him to see the results. Stockdale did as requested by his Committee colleagues, the Earl noting that Stockdale was 'most enthusiastic' regarding the railway.

By November 1839 Burlington realised that the West Cumberland Railway was even closer to becoming a reality. Whilst on a walk to Old Park, overlooking the Leven estuary, Burlington pointed out to Currey what he would want should the scheme be successful. Currey, however, didn't anticipate anything being submitted to Parliament that session.

Our story now turns to other schemes and to London. Whilst Hague and Rastrick were busy surveying, and support was building up along the Cumbrian Coast, there had been stirrings in the House of Commons that would have significant impact on Cumbria's coastal railway.

On 7 June 1838 a motion had been put forward in the Commons asking that a Commission to inquire into the best line of railway from London and the manufacturing districts of England to Edinburgh and Glasgow. That motion was amended to remove the reference to the 'manufacturing districts' (i.e. Leeds, Manchester and Liverpool districts) and passed. Despite the West Cumberland Railway committee's petition to the Government mentioned above, it was not until 14 August 1839 that the Commons voted to set up an inquiry and report into the merits of the projected lines between London and Edinburgh and Glasgow: via York, Newcastle-upon-Tyne and Berwick; via York, Newcastle and Hexham; via Lancaster, Whitehaven and Carlisle; and via Lancaster, Penrith and Carlisle. The inquiry was to also consider the two lines from London to York, by Derby and Rotherham, and by Cambridge and Lincoln. When compared with existing transportation needs there was no need for rival or duplicate routes between towns, especially between London and Glasgow and Edinburgh! Such was the novelty of railways at that time.

Whilst the West Cumberland route was to be considered against the rival route via Penrith, it was seen by the West Cumberland Railway Provisional Committee that regarding their line as a trunk route from London to the Scottish cities alone was insufficient a reason to favour it. It was necessary to consider its benefit as a connection between 'the manufacturing districts' of South-East Lancashire and the

West Riding of Yorkshire, and Northern Ireland via Whitehaven and Belfast, as well as Glasgow and Edinburgh. A petition was quickly presented to Parliament in the name of Lewis Cubitt, who had now become Chairman. This asked that the inquiry and report should include the merits of the route from the manufacturing districts. A motion to this effect was put to the house on the following day. The additional benefits would be considered.

Until recent years, and certainly at this time, it was necessary for the promoters of a railway to deposit their plans, with other information, with the Private Bill Office of the House of Commons. In order to obtain their Act, this had to be done by the end of November for consideration in the coming parliamentary session. Additionally a notice of the intention to apply for an Act and all relevant plans had to be deposited with Clerk of the Peace of the counties through which the line would pass. Each affected parish had to be served notice, and receive relevant plans. It was necessary for two copies of the notice to be posted on the parish church door over three successive weeks before the plans were deposited with Parliament, thus allowing everyone affected to make their objections via their representatives or, should they have a seat in either house, directly when the Bill was subsequently reviewed. We know that Francis Yarker and his partner, John Postlethwaite, posted notices at Colton, Cartmel, Lancaster, Heysham, Bolton, Warton and Beetham parish churches on 3, 10 and 17 November 1839.

With the plans deposited, it was then necessary for the Provisional Committee to follow their Bill's progress through parliament. If that were not enough, they had to follow the inquiry of the Royal Commission of Peter Barlow and Sir Frederick Smith. The Commissioners reported twice. Their second report, presented to the Commons on 19 May 1840, was the nail in the coffin for the West Cumberland Railway scheme – they recommended the Penrith route. They also believed that there was little likelihood of sufficient traffic to justify even that scheme.

Despite their closely following progress of the Bill, it seems to have taken a while for the full impact of the report to be realised by the Ulverston promoters. Edward Dawson was corresponding with Hague and Stockdale on the outcome of the Commissioners report and the possibility of a land reclamation company. On 25 July Yarker wrote to Stockdale offering some consolation by means of alternative schemes, whilst pointing out that most of Ulverston's townsmen had gone cold on the subject.

It appears from the communications I have received from town, that the Commrs report has put an extinguisher upon our Railway project as it at present stands. We do not however quite despair - we have a notion that if we cannot accomplish our object, according to our existing plan, it may be ultimately effected in another way - We conceive it to be quite practicable to compass a Railway communication between Whitehaven and Rampside across the River Duddon, and to get on with great facility from Rampside to Fleetwood, by means of Steamers. If this be done we consider that the promoters of the line from Lancaster inland, will be chalked off that scheme, and if so, that the parties interested in the Lancaster Railway will seek . . . an outlet for their traffic, become zealous supporters of the Bay undertaking, and that many other persons who are now sceptical as to the feasibility of the scheme, will, after witnessing the success of the works over the Duddon, be made to see the practicability and advantage of embanking & forming a Railway across the Bay of Morecambe. It is possible too that when the Ulverstone people perceive the stream of Traffic giving them the go bye, they may be roused from their unaccountable apathy, into a befitting sense

of what is due to their own interests, and become as strong supporters of our plan, as they are now indifferent to it. We might either push forward the railway between Whitehaven and Rampside leaving the embankment on the Bay until afterwards, or endeavour to have a separate company formed for the embankment, and so attempt to carry on both parts of the scheme at once, or we may try to accomplish the embankment of the Bays, as a separate undertaking for the sake of the land reclaimed irrespective of a railway. In any plan which proposes to connect the Railway and Fleetwood we may calculate with certainty the assistance of Sir H Fleetwood, and the parties interested in the Fleetwood Railway, and I believe Lord Burlington is favourably disposed towards the establishment of a Railway, which would connect itself with Fleetwood. The embankment across the Bay as a separate and independent undertaking is now a subject of consideration, among our friends in London, and if the views of the Landowners and the other parties locally interested, are found to be favourable towards the plan, I have no doubt an endeavour will be made to form a company with every chance of success. Our Whitehaven friends are very anxious to effect the immediate accomplishment of the other part of the project, and I have no reason to believe, that if it be found that the water passage can be made, with certainty and regularity, the plan will be pushed forward, under very favourable auspices. You have given the business so much consideration, that you will be able to afford us very valuable advice, as to the most desirable plan of proceeding, and it would give me much pleasure, if you would be kind enough to favor me with your views as to the various plans which have suggested themselves as worthy of attention. If you could see Lord Burlington on the subject, and ascertain how he stands affected with regards to it, and especially, as to the embankment of the Bay, which I look upon as the main object to be accomplished, it would be very serviceable in determining our system of operations.

I am certain you will do your best to aid us, and that we may rely on your best exertions in favour of the cause, in which we have been labouring so long and hitherto so unsuccessfully.

Yarker was right with his assertions that thoughts would now turn to linking Furness with mainland Lancashire via Fleetwood. John Power of the Preston & Wyre Railway had been in contact with him that June. The Preston & Wyre line opened in the following month to Fleetwood, from where steamers were already running to Ardrossan for Glasgow and to Bardsea for Ulverston. John Abel Smith, MP, a former banker and land speculator, bought Roa Island, on the southern tip of Furness. If there was going to be a steamer port in Furness to connect with a railway north, it would be off Roa Island in the deep water channel known as Piel Harbour.

It was to be another three years before a railway was again mooted from Maryport and on through Whitehaven to the south. By now Sir Fleming Senhouse was dead. This time Lord Lowther, heir to the Lonsdale estates, was to be the figurehead. On the assumption that the destination would be Roa Island, Smith tried in 1841-2 to get Parliamentary sanction to allow him to control the waters for a significant area around Piel Harbour. Since this affected ancient rights to the harbour of refuge of Piel harbour, that Bill failed. In the following year he was more successful when he obtained a Parliamentary authority to build a causeway from Rampside out to his island and a pier into the deep waters of Piel harbour with the Pile Pier Act of 27 June 1843.

Meanwhile in Furness, railways of a more local nature were being suggested to Lord Burlington. These would connect the quarries at Kirkby and haematite mines above Dalton with Rampside and the iron merchant's wharves on the tidal Barrow channel. As George Stephenson's men were surveying the Whitehaven Junction Railway from Maryport to Whitehaven, Messrs McClean and Wright were surveying the Furness Railway on behalf of the Lord Burlington's engineers, Walker and Burges. Both lines were authorised in the 1843-4 session of Parliament.

The railway between these schemes, the Whitehaven & Furness Junction Railway, would not be surveyed until 1844, in time for the 1844-5 session. By this time Lowther had succeeded his father as Earl of Lonsdale and his W&FJR from Whitehaven to Kirkby Ireleth received parliamentary approval in the summer of 1845. Locke's Shap route also received parliamentary authority in that session, in the guise of the Lancaster & Carlisle Railway, as did the Kendal & Windermere Railway.

This time there was significant support from Burlington and his supporters for the coast railway. Interest was also shown from Manchester, with banking partners Samuel Cunliffe and Samuel Brookes among the investors. Most significant of those subscribing to the scheme was a prosperous railway and general contractor from Sale, Cheshire, by the name of John Brogden. His subscription for £40,000 worth of shares outshone all other subscribers, including Lonsdale himself. This was the height of the railway mania.

With the W&FJR and Furness Railway authorised, railways could soon connect Whitehaven with Rampside and Dalton. An immediate, if roundabout, through route was now close to fruition from London to Belfast, via Fleetwood, Roa Island and Whitehaven pending the

Furness extending its line north-eastwards to Ulverston and the W&FJR bridging the gap to Lancaster. With these completed, a through rail link from London to Whitehaven would be achieved and Whitehaven would become the Packet station for Belfast.

The townsmen of Ulverston were again talking favourably about the railway to Lancaster and the benefits it could give, and they were none to keen on the Furness Railway. The Furness, by serving the wharves at Barrow, was diverting traffic and trade from Ulverston. To make things worse, the canal was again suffering from the river Leven changing its course away from its entrance gates.

There was talk of land reclamation in the Leven estuary and of a channel to Greenodd. During the summer of 1843, Richard Roper of the Newland Furnace had written to his neighbour, John Fell junior (better known as the contractor and engineer John Barraclough Fell who owned wharves and a sawmill at Greenodd), regarding reclamation of land in the Leven estuary. Benjamin Currey was also in correspondence with Roper regarding the schemes, the making of a canal to Greenodd and of the objections of John Morritt, the owner of the western shore of the estuary. Currey was representing Burlington, who owned the eastern shore. The word was that, although a subscription list existed, no scheme would be put to Parliament that session. They were discussing Roper and Fell's Ulverston & Greenodd Navigation and Land Redemption Company. This planned to reclaim a large section of the Leven estuary below Greenodd and build a canal from Greenodd towards Ulverston, thus improving access to the Greenodd wharves. In the summer of 1845 the Greenodd men went as far as proposing the purchase of the Ulverston Canal.

The Ulverston men were actually split over which railway to support beyond Ulverston, for there was more

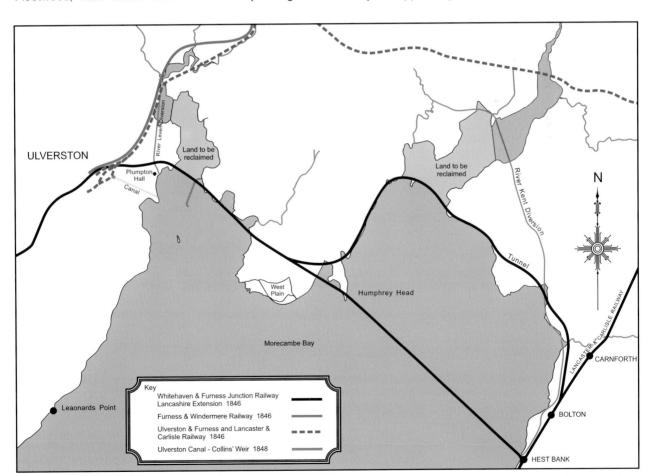

The Lancashire Extension Railway of the Whitehaven & Furness Junction Railway. *This was one of the rival schemes for connecting Furness with the Lancaster & Carlisle Railway. As can be seen, two possible routes were submitted, with the idea that if one failed the other might succeed. The Ulverstone Canal Company saw through this and used it as a basis for objection. That and bungled documentation being submitted to Parliament led to the scheme failing Parliamentary scrutiny.*

(Based on Deposited Plans, redrawn by Alan Johnstone)

than one scheme this time around! Two were aimed at putting Whitehaven on the through route to Northern Ireland, whilst the others would link Furness with the existing railways south.

One was the Furness & Windermere scheme, effectively an extension of the Kendal & Windermere Railway, via the eastern shore of Windermere and Newby Bridge to Ulverston. This would give a very roundabout link from Ulverston to the growing national railway system. The Secretary of the Furness & Windermere Railway was John B Fell of Sparkbridge with Thomas Roper of the Newland Ironworks as a Director. Coincidentally Roper and Fell were Chairman and Secretary to the Windermere Steamboat Company, which had started running passenger steamers on Windermere in 1845. By building this railway they would secure the interests of their businesses.

The second was the Ulverstone & Milnthorpe Union Railway. This was largely supported by Ulster linen merchants, although its engineer had links to the L&CR in a junior capacity. Its purpose was to link Ulster with the cotton towns of Lancashire, via a steamship service to Whitehaven.

The third was the Lancaster & Carlisle Railway's Ulverston & Furness and Lancaster & Carlisle Railway. This was for a line from Milnthorpe, via Newby Bridge to Ulverston, thus giving the L&CR control of the potentially lucrative railway traffic to Furness and Whitehaven. The engineers were Joseph Locke and J E Errington, engineers to the L&CR. Locke was keen to point out that this line would avoid any difficulties with navigation in the Leven and Kent estuaries but didn't press the point that his route involved a long tunnel.

Finally there was the W&FJR's Lancashire Extension Railway, which would run around the coast from Dalton – later Ulverston – to Bolton (le-Sands). This scheme also allowed for land reclamation in Morecambe Bay.

It was the two latter schemes that were to be the cause of the split in loyalties in Ulverston.

Lord Burlington could see that one scheme or other had a chance of succeeding and needed some influence over those, which would affect his estates. Benjamin Currey became involved in both the L&CR's and W&FJR's schemes.

The W&FJR proposal would affect the course of the river Leven north of Ulverston Canal. Intriguingly Stephenson proposed to build two embankments in the Leven estuary. One was to be south from Mereness Point to the western shore, and another, to carry the railway, from just north of Tridley Point on the western shore across to Capeshead Point, thus creating a significant area of arable land where the tidal river once flowed. The Leven would be diverted in a navigable channel across country from just above the northern embankment down to a point between Tridley Point and Plumpton Hall. This all sounded like the Ulverston & Greenodd Navigation scheme!

Whilst this would be of great benefit to Greenodd, which would gain a canal instead of the shallow upper channel of the Leven, it would adversely affect navigation to the canal gates. The scouring effect of the ebb tide from the upper Leven estuary would be removed if it were reduced to a canal, thus leading to the silting up of the channel at Canal Foot. Scared, the Ulverston Canal Navigation proprietors called in a Scots engineer, James Leslie, to review the situation. Leslie reported back in February 1846, pointing out that the W&FJR scheme would lead to the reclamation of 960 acres of the Leven estuary with the potential loss of 209 million cubic feet of water to scour the estuary at the Canal Foot at spring tides. Yarker drafted a memorial to the Admiralty, objecting to the proposed railway and its likely impact on navigation. The memorial also pointed out that the W&FJR scheme was effectively a hybrid Bill: two separate Bills were being deposited concurrently – one for the railway and the other for the Morecambe Bay embankment. If one failed then the other could still succeed. This was totally against

Parliamentary standing orders. The Canal company favoured the L&CR scheme!

Surprisingly, two railways were proposed on the submitted plans. One line following George Stephenson's 1838 route through (yes, through) Ulverston, down to the coast at Plumpton, and across past Capes Head and to the south of Cark and Flookburgh to Humphrey Head, where it headed across Morecambe Bay to join the Lancaster & Carlisle Railway at Hest Bank. The other left the above line south of Flookburgh to head across north of Humphrey Head, and just inland of the shore up to Grange. From here it was to cross the Kent estuary on the embankment described above, running just inland of the shore past Silverdale and Carnforth to join the L&CR line at Bolton.

Not only would the Leven be affected. In order that land could be reclaimed in the Kent estuary, it was proposed that the river Winster would be diverted from a point where it is crossed by the modern A590 Lindale Bypass to the Kent estuary just north of Ulpha Point. Just to the south there was to be one of two embankments across the Kent estuary, running south to Arnside. The other, carrying the railway, was to run from Blawith Point, near Grange, around the north side of Holme island and then south east to below Arnside. The Kent (and Winster) were to be diverted along another navigable channel which was to follow the course of the later Ulverstone & Lancaster railway, crossing the railway south of Silverdale and running on parallel to the proposed railway and parallel to the Lancaster & Carlisle line past Bolton (le-Sands) to reach the sea after passing under the second embankment (from Humphrey Head) at Hest Bank.

Three of the four schemes were submitted to parliament in November 1845 – the Ulverston & Milnthorpe Union scheme appears to have been abandoned beforehand. The Ulverston & Furness and Lancaster & Carlisle scheme was withdrawn in May 1846, due to the requisite investment capital not having been raised, whilst the Lancashire Extension Railway fell foul of parliamentary standing orders. As realised by the Ulverston Canal proprietors, it was a hybrid bill for both a railway and for land reclamation. The engineers, in their rush to meet parliamentary deadlines, had mixed up their plans for the two parts of the scheme making it hard to work out what the envisaged railway route was!

Thus the second phase of activity to build a railway from Furness to mainland Lancashire came to an unsuccessful end. The W&FJR took a while to give up on the scheme; even as late as November 1846 Burlington met their engineer, Robert Stephenson, on the Leven Sands. However nothing was to come of it for the moment.

In Ulverston, Francis Yarker and the Ulverston canal proprietors could rest easy for a while and focus on building up trade to the canal. As already mentioned, the canal was suffering because the Leven channel was flowing east of Chapel Island and thus the entry channel to the canal was silted up. They realised that to continue trading with any success, the river must be made to run closer to Canal Foot.

In early 1848 they again approached James Leslie, who supplied a plan to build a stone breakwater from Park Head to Black Scar, a prominent rock outcrop in the sands to the north of Chapel Island. The construction contract was given to George Collins of Lancaster. This action proved effective for even before the embankment was completed, in December 1848, the estuary was silting up around the breakwater and the channel was again running close to the canal gates. 1848 saw the canal handle what was to prove to be its largest annual tonnage of cargoes.

What Yarker and his allies couldn't stop was the steady increase in trade at the upstart harbour at Barrow. The growing output of Furness iron ore was being funnelled by the Furness Railway to the piers in the Barrow channel with little going through their canal.

The Ulverstone & Lancaster Railway

3

AFTER THE FAILURE to get a railway built east from Furness in 1846, circumstances dictated that the neither the W&FJR nor the Furness were in a position to consider raising the subject again. The W&FJR was having trouble getting its own line funded, having to replace its plan for a Duddon viaduct with the less risky option of joining the Furness near Broughton. Meanwhile the Furness itself was, despite its apparent prosperity, having financial difficulties of its own. It needed to concentrate on its core business of transporting ore and slate to Barrow. It was to be an independent promoter, with much experience in the building and management of railways, who would lead the completion of the missing link.

John Brogden was a wealthy man with money to invest. He first showed an interest in Furness in 1845. In that year he unsuccessfully tendered for the contract to construct the Furness Railway. Later that year, as we have seen, he became the major subscriber to the Whitehaven & Furness Junction Railway. Whether Brogden and his Manchester neighbours followed through that intention with the purchase of shares is unknown. In 1846 he subscribed to the FR's Broughton extension. Possibly through this work he became a friend of John R McClean, the FR Engineer.

At about the same time Brogden invested in the South Eastern Railway. He invested enough money to be elected a Director of that company and remained so until about 1850. During those years, from 1845 to 1850, Brogden was successfully running several businesses: cleaning the streets of Manchester and providing horses to the local authority; running a similar operation in London; buying, selling and hiring horses (the source of his wealth); and as a railway contractor, by this time in partnership with his eldest son, John. His railway construction work was largely in Lancashire as well as contracts in Cambridgeshire, Kent, Norfolk and elsewhere.

In about 1850, and coincidental with his departure (in some disgrace) from the SER, John Brogden's interests returned to Furness. One of the first things he did was to invest in the iron mines. He acquired mineral leases for mines, at Stainton at least. His son, John, bought Lowfield House, a farm at Lindal, in the haematite ore field and conveniently close to the likely course of the FR if it extended from Lindal to Ulverston. Shares were bought in the Ulverston Mining Company, who had mines at Lindal Cote. On a grander scale the Brogden's bought Lightburn, a mansion on the southern edge of Ulverston, from William Gale. John (junior) made it his home, joining in with the local society, subscribing to good causes when they arose and preaching for the local Wesleyan Methodists. John Brogden (junior) was to manage the family businesses in Furness until his untimely death, of a brain haemorrhage, on 6 November 1855.

John Brogden also made moves to provide the final link in the railway around the Cumbrian Coast. He was fully aware of the W&FJR plans and how they had failed, and through his friend McClean he knew that the FR had no intention, beyond extending to Ulverston, of filling the void across Morecambe Bay. It was building up a nice business serving the iron mines and transporting the ore to the wharves at Barrow.

As noted above, John (junior) was already settling into Ulverston society. A relationship was built up with Henry Kennedy, doctor of law, London barrister, son of the Ulverston mine owner Charles Storr Kennedy, and shareholder in the Ulverston Mining Company and Ulverston Canal Navigation. The Brogdens would use Dr Kennedy in their dealings with local landowners when it became time to purchase land for the proposed railway.

The Brogdens took on FR Engineers McClean & Stileman, FR Solicitor (and Burlington's Steward) William Currey and FR Secretary James Ramsden in the same roles for their proposed railway. During the summer of 1850, George H Saunders, for McClean & Stileman, surveyed the route for a railway from Ulverston to the Lancaster & Carlisle Railway. The route proposed was to run from the FR terminus above Ulverston eastwards on a gradient of 1 in 60, crossing the canal with an opening bridge and otherwise leaving only 7 ft. 6 in. headroom. It continued on the level past Plumpton, crossing the Leven on a 737-yard-long wooden viaduct with a 30 ft. opening bridge before skirting the coast to Cark. It then ran to the north of Winder Moor before heading around the coast to Grange. From here the route was to embank the Winster estuary from Blawith Point to Meathop Point and continue on, over another 737-yard-long wooden viaduct with opening span, to Arnside. From here, rather than following the coast, the route was to be inland to the east of Silverdale and on to the L&CR at Carnforth.

The presence of the surveyor seems not to have aroused suspicions from the townsfolk of Ulverston – perhaps they were used to this by now. The columns of the Ulverston Advertiser include letters suggesting that a railway would be a good thing, but it was only in the period leading up to the application to Parliament that it was revealed that the Brogdens were proposing to build the railway. In July 1850, the Ulverston Advertiser commented on a report on the Iron Ore Trade of Great Britain by Braithwaite Poole, a Traffic Manager for the LNWR: this specifically quoted the amount of haematite that could be potentially sent by rail if only a link from Furness to the main line railways existed. To the modern mind it would appear that the Brogdens were feeding Stephen Soulby the editorial material he needed!

Since it was again proposed to cross the Leven on a viaduct and embankment, passing close to Holker Hall, objections would be likely from the Ulverston Canal proprietors and the Earl of Burlington. In May 1850, McClean and Ramsden, with Park of the L&CR, called on Burlington to discuss the building of a railway past the Holker estate. Burlington would be well aware by now that such a scheme was inevitable, but the presence of Park suggests either that the L&CR were considering a line from Ulverston to their railway or were supportive of Brogden's plans. As for opposition from the Canal company, Brogden was prepared. In November 1850, when the announcement was made for the proposed application to Parliament for the Ulverstone & Lancaster Railway, another advertisement appeared in the newspapers. The proprietors of the Ulverston Canal Navigation advertised their Canal for sale – to anyone except a railway company! This would prevent the Furness, W&FJR, Kendal & Windermere or L&CR from blocking the Brogden scheme. John Brogden was, of course, a private individual and thus, probably according to his plans, bought the entire shareholding of the Canal Company.

The promotion of the U&LR led the Kendal & Windermere Railway to revive their Furness & Windermere Railway scheme, with the addition of a branch from Haverthwaite, along the eastern shore of the Leven estuary, to join the planned U&LR. Although announcements were made alongside those of the Ulverston & Lancaster, the scheme was dropped before it could be submitted to Parliament.

In November 1850 the necessary activities were carried out to get the Ulverstone & Lancaster Railway Bill raised in Parliament. The subscription contract listed the provisional committee of the Duke of Buccleuch, the Earl of Burlington, R W Lumley and Joseph Paxton (all FR investors and

John Brogden (1798 – 1869) in later life. *Founder and principle shareholder of the Ulverstone & Lancaster Railway Company, he built up a significant business empire, such that by the time of his death he was probably a millionaire.*
(Courtesy Grange-over-Sands Photographic Society)

William Cavendish (1808-1891), 2nd Earl of Burlington and 7th Duke of Devonshire, photographed in 1863. *Although a passive bystander in the earlier railway schemes, after 1848 he was the active Chairman of the Furness Railway Company and supporter of the U&LR. Together with the Duke of Buccleuch, Devonshire aided the Brogdens in 1856 by lending money to the U&LR on behalf of the FR. This was at a time when borrowing from usual sources proved difficult.* *(Courtesy National Portrait Gallery)*

James Brunlees (1816-1892). *Whilst McClean & Stileman prepared the Parliamentary plans for the U&LR, they resigned in 1853. It was Brunlees who revised the plans for the embankments and viaducts, supervised their construction and ensured the success of the project.*
(Courtesy Institution of Civil Engineers)

Directors), William Gale and Henry Kennedy (representing Ulverston investment) and the Brogden family (John, John jnr, Alexander and James Garstang). The principal subscriber was of course John Brogden, with a recorded intention of investing £100,000 of the £220,000 required. His son John intended to invest a further £54,000.

The Bill's passage through Parliament was relatively smooth. It came before the Parliamentary committee on 13–15 May 1851. Lord Burlington and Sir Joseph Paxton, together with Stephen Jackson of Ulverston gave evidence in favour of the Bill. Objections were raised by Messrs Roper over the proposed tolls for mineral traffic and by the 'inhabitants of Ulverston' who wanted to ensure the Leven channel ran close to Canal Foot by having the opening span on the Leven viaduct located at the western end. The former was over-ruled and the latter decision left to the Admiralty. L&CR Engineer J E Errington gave evidence that the site of the opening span would have little influence on the channel at Canal Foot and that the presence of the viaduct would probably deepen the channel. As might be expected, the Admiralty requested that the navigation of the Kent and Leven rivers should be preserved by the provision of opening spans in the viaducts there and that some protection be made for Ulverston as a port. There was some discussion over the provision of foot access over both viaducts; the company didn't want this. The committee insisted that a footway be provided only over the Leven for a small toll. The U&LR Act received Royal Assent on 24 July 1851. The bells of St Mary's rang a 'merry peal' across Ulverston on the following day.

John Brogden was an established investor in railways. We have heard of his involvement with the South Eastern Railway, where he represented Manchester shareholders for several years. Whilst the U&LR was under construction, he was involved with schemes with engineer John McClean. In 1851 McClean famously became the first individual to gain parliamentary authority to lease a railway: the South Staffordshire Railway for whom he was engineer. According to G P Neele, later Superintendent of the Line for the LNWR and working for the SSR at the time, McClean left the management of the railway to the Brogdens. Alexander Brogden became the Manager of the railway whilst his brother Henry became Locomotive Superintendent. Their involvement in that line continued until 1861, when McClean gave up the lease and the SSR was leased instead to the LNWR. When the railway opened, much of the ore carried over the U&LR would be heading for South Staffordshire. In the 1850s both McClean and John Brogden (senior) would separately approach the FR Board and propose a similar lease.

One of McLean's achievements whilst leasing the SSR was to promote the South Staffordshire Water Company, to take fresh, clean water from Lichfield, at the eastern end of the SSR, through pipes running alongside the SSR to industrial Dudley, where the water was said to be foul. In Furness, Ulverston still relied on streams and wells for its water supply. Aware of this, in 1851, Messrs Brogden and McClean proposed an Ulverston Waterworks Company. The scheme was similar but smaller to the South Staffordshire Waterworks scheme in that a reservoir would be built above Pennington and the water from there would be piped alongside the Furness Railway's Ulverston extension and the western end of the U&LR as far as the canal. Whilst the Staffordshire scheme succeeded (and the company existed into modern times), the townsfolk of Ulverston wanted their own scheme, to be controlled by the council. Following the announcements in the Ulverston Advertiser in November 1851 that the two schemes were to be put to Parliament, negotiations followed, common sense prevailed and the town scheme went ahead, although it was notable that a pipe would specifically serve the Brogden farm at Lowfield House. Excess water was to be discharged into the canal at no cost to the Canal Company.

Whilst establishing themselves in Furness, the Brogdens also took an interest in the coal and iron industries of South Wales. By 1853 they were taking out mineral leases in the

Ogmore, Llynvi and Garw valleys, including several existing coal mines. In the following year they acquired the lease of the Tondu Ironworks where John Brogden's fourth son, James, was installed as Manager. Furness ore would be shipped by sea to the Tondu works, via Porthcawl, for many years.

The Furness Railway company was not in a position to promote expensive lines itself and neither had it the will. In the 1850s it saw itself primarily as a carrier of minerals: iron ore and slate to the piers and wharves at Barrow. It had supported the W&FJR scheme of 1846 for a line from Whitehaven to the L&CR (or at least regretted its failure), which would have utilised a few miles of the Furness from Ireleth to Ulverston. However, it had no enthusiasm to extend its own lines beyond Broughton and Ulverston. It was unfortunate that in its first years of operation, the FR had difficulties in keeping its house in order. The principal shareholders were to be kept unaware that whilst the amount of ore flowing to Barrow was increasing, the operating costs were growing even faster. All came to light in August 1848 when the company Chairman, Benjamin Currey (Steward for the Earl of Burlington and other Cavendish families) died. Burlington was quickly elected to the Board and made Chairman. Suddenly all was revealed to the FR's key investor. Immediate cost-cutting reforms were instigated, including work on the extension from Crooklands to Lindal for 12 months. By 1850, the FR was showing a genuine profit again, but it was still cautious to extend even to Ulverston without there being someone else committing to building a line on towards Lancaster.

One of the first acts of the Brogdens following the passing of the U&LR Act in July 1851 was to set up a Board of Directors. No longer having a need for nobility and connections in Parliament, John Brogden restricted his board to himself, his three eldest sons, John, Alexander and Henry, and James Garstang. Garstang was a Manchester businessman and father-in-law to both John (junior) and Alexander Brogden! All was kept in the family. At the following day's Board meeting, on 9 August 1851, the main officers were confirmed as before; Ramsden as Secretary with McClean and Stileman as Engineers. Messrs J & W Norris were appointed Solicitors jointly with William Currey and J R Bevan appointed as Bookkeeper.

Construction of the railway was to be carried out in a number of contracts, many of which would be undertaken by the Brogdens themselves. These were:

No. 1   Carnforth, junction with L&CR to Arnside;

No. 2   Fighting Cocks embankment (east end of Kent viaduct to mainland at Arnside);

No. 3   Kent Viaduct;

No. 4   Meathop Embankment (Blawith Point to Kent Viaduct);

No. 5   Blawith Point (near Grange) to Wyke;

No. 6   Wyke (near Humphrey Head) to Cark;

No. 7   Capeshead Embankment (Cark to east end of Leven Viaduct);

No. 8   Leven Viaduct;

No. 9   Tridley (West end of Leven Viaduct) to Canal Viaduct (east end);

No. 10   Ulverston, Canal Viaduct to junction with FR.

Construction would be phased, with the most difficult sections (the Capeshead and Meathop embankments) being given priority. However, it was the westernmost contract that commenced first, taking advantage of the excess materials to be dug out for the FR's Ulverston extension.

Whilst this was underway, negotiations were started with the Duchy of Lancaster for rights to acquire land and build the railway in the river estuaries around Morecambe Bay. In February 1853, McClean & Stileman resigned from their position as Engineers to the company, being replaced by James Brunlees, an engineer with some experience of building sea embankments for railways. Whilst the Directors' Minutes suggest that the Brogdens were getting frustrated by delays in their Engineers supplying the necessary plans, one must assume that the resignation was by mutual agreement since McClean and the Brogdens were still in partnership elsewhere. This wasn't the first resignation from the employ of the U&LR. Some disagreement must have occurred in the five months following their appointment since on 20 January 1852 William Currey had tendered his resignation as one of the Solicitors to the company. This was read to the Board at their next meeting, on 16 February, and accepted. It was recorded that the Directors regretted the circumstances mentioned by Currey. Messrs Norris remained as Solicitors, although they would be joined in later years by Messrs Tahourdin.

Once the U&LR looked to be a serious possibility, the Furness Railway decided, finally, to complete its line to Ulverston. Although authorised in 1846, construction was postponed once before being stopped at Lindal: after all there were few active iron mines beyond that place. The route followed to Ulverston was to cost the Furness and its successors. After crossing the Lowfield House estate on an embankment the line wound its way down through Pennington to a terminus above Ulverston, on what is now the southern end of Prince's Street, thus giving some relief to the otherwise steep gradients. The Ulverston townsfolk had, sensibly, expected the railway to terminate near the canal, but that appears to have been too much for the Furness and their station was built 113 feet above sea level. McClean was left with the problem of getting the U&LR down to sea level at Plumpton. If the junction had been end-on, then the U&L, as authorised, would have commenced with a severe 1 in 60 incline for the first mile. Instead he moved the junction with the existing FR line a quarter of a mile nearer Lindal, effectively at the station throat, allowing the gradients to be reduced to a maximum of 1 in 76. The FR built the first quarter mile from this junction to join the U&LR at the Prince's Street bridge.

Henry Kennedy busied himself that summer negotiating to buy the land required for the first section of the U&LR from the FR junction to the canal. On 10 November 1851 the first sod of the U&LR was cut to the west of Lightburn Terrace, on land bought from Rev. Tolming of Coniston. The Ulverston Advertiser hoped for speedy progress on the construction. They could hope, but to the dismay of many it was to be almost six years before a train would run between Ulverston and Carnforth.

There's an irony in the choice of location for that event since Rev. Tolming believed he had received insufficient compensation for the land he sold to the railway. He took the railway to court, culminating in a Special Jury, made up of Liverpool tradesmen, gathering in the Victoria Concert Hall, Ulverston on 24 August 1853. They decided for the parson, generously awarding him £426 9s 0d for his 2843 square yards of land plus £150 severance (for splitting his land in two). That is, he received £726 10s 0d per acre! The Brogdens can't have been amused, since most landowners were getting half that.

Sense prevailed on the construction of the section of line down to the Canal. Agreement was made that the contract would be an extension of the FR's Ulverston contract. Contractor George Boulton could thus use the soil from the Pennington and Lightburn Terrace cuttings to build the embankment down to the Canal.

Once construction was under way the Brogdens thought little of the niceties of keeping records of their Board meetings. After all, all the directors were in the family. The only exception in the early days was when Sir Joseph Paxton was co-opted to the board on 15 November 1851. Paxton, gardener and friend of the 6th Duke of Devonshire and director of several railways, had been recently knighted for his successful involvement with the Crystal Palace. Intriguingly he had resigned from the Furness Board in the previous month. For whatever reason he didn't stay long on the U&LR board. He attended two board meetings (10 and 11 December 1851) but there is no record of his being ratified as a Director by the shareholders.

The Brogdens could be said to be quite bullish about their position. They were so confident that in late 1851 they actually proposed to lease the Furness Railway, in the same way that John McClean had leased the South Staffordshire Railway. In fact McClean had made such an offer himself some time earlier. Brogden and McClean had the support of FR director Joseph Paxton, who possibly moved from the FR to the ascendant U&LR in order to stay involved with what would be the controlling company. Fortunately for the FR shareholders, their board declined the offer but were to agree to invest in the U&LR project themselves. This may have been why Paxton disappeared from the railway scene in Furness: he could hardly ask for his seat back on the FR board, where he had already been replaced by a Burlington man, Stephen Eddy (manager of Burlington's mines and quarries in the north). Such a lease would have given the Brogdens income whilst building their line. As it was, the Brogdens would have to await completion before they would have any income to pay off debts and dividends.

Although construction of the U&LR had, apparently, started quite promptly, the first section of line down to the canal progressed slowly and was dependent on progress on the FR's Ulverston line. The first of the over-bridges in the section, over the Dragley Road (modern Victoria Road) was completed in January 1852 but collapsed the following March. A temporary bridge allowed the contractor's engine to bring spoil down from Pennington to continue the embankment down to the canal whilst the permanent bridge was rebuilt. It would be November 1853 before the masons could start on the foundations of the six-arch canal viaduct. At the same time as the work on the viaduct, a new basin was dug to where the various depots could be moved, saving the need for ships to lower their masts to reach the basin at the Canal Head. A warehouse was provided, but otherwise only an ore depot was set up alongside the basin, with the ore being delivered by road. The slipway there pre-dated the new basin.

Work on the sea embankments themselves started in April-May 1853 in two places. One was the Meathop embankment between Meathop Point and Blawith Point, near Grange. The other was westward from Cark, the Capeshead embankment. It was on this embankment that several river bridges were eliminated. The Capeshead embankment started about quarter of a mile inland from where the river Eea enters Morecambe Bay, crossing that river almost immediately, the river flowing from north-east to south-west. After passing the site of an old shipyard, the river then looped back to the north before flowing south-west into the Bay at Cark Marsh, skirting a coal wharf on the shore. To avoid the need for bridges, the river was diverted to run parallel to and south of the railway, which cut through the afore-mentioned wharf. This embankment would cross only one small stream by a tidal sluice as it skirted the eastern shore of the Leven estuary, and moved past the headlands of Quarry Flat point, Ravensbarrow Point and Capes Head before heading west across the estuary to Tridley Point and Plumpton. Lord Burlington was to be the beneficiary of the reclaimed land here.

Along with the embankments to carry the railway, weirs and breakwaters were built to guide the course of the Leven and Kent rivers to the viaduct sites. These breakwaters ran for some length both upstream and downstream of the viaducts. Their other purpose was to protect the railway embankments from being undermined by the action of the rivers. As noted by Stockdale in an earlier chapter, damage from a river would be more devastating to an embankment than the mere actions of a high tide.

Work on the embankments started slowly and was often held back as repairs were made to the damage following storms and high tides. One reason for the initial slow progress was the use of wheelbarrows and men to transfer sand from the shore to the embankments. It wasn't until September 1853 that a shortage of labour led to this work being performed by two-wheeled carts hauled by horses.

Brunlees claimed that little work was done in the winter months, but from the diary of Brogden's farm manager and general factotum, James Stelfox, it would appear that this was not the case, certainly in the later years.

Navvies arrived in May 1852 on completion of Brogden's sub-contracts on the Great Northern Railway between Peterborough and Retford. They set up camp at Meathop, on the Westmorland side of the river Winster. Perhaps Brogden's experience on contracts on the Middle Levels of Norfolk came into play here. The deposited plans failed to show how the Winster would be crossed, it flowing at that time in the middle of Winster Bay. The navvies' first job was to divert the Winster in a new fixed channel from the existing sea wall adjacent to the Castlehead mansion to a place adjacent to Meathop Fell, where the river would pass under the railway through a tidal sluice. Although this differed from the four-arch bridge authorised in the U&LR Act, it proved to be a sensible substitution and wasn't questioned when the railway was later inspected by the Board of Trade. A breakwater was built out into the Kent estuary to prevent that river from silting up the Winster. The railway would cut through the tip of Meathop Fell in a narrow cutting. With the river diverted, Brogden, through his acquisition of the Meathop Marsh estate and Holme Island, gained several hundred acres of potentially prime farmland, now partly taken up by the Grange-over-Sands Golf Club.

Work on the embankment across the Winster Bay started in May 1853, led by contractor William Hanson, but it would be November 1854 before the Earl of Burlington observed that the embankment was anything close to being completed, with a push on to achieve this before the next high tides. Two factors hampered progress, both here and on the other embankments across the estuaries: the tides and the 'holes' left following diversion of the rivers.

Whilst the engineers of earlier schemes (George Stephenson and Hague) had proposed their embankments to be of solid stone construction, around which silting would provide protection from undercutting by the tides, Brunlees' embankments were of similar construction to those he recently designed for the Londonderry and Coleraine Railway. In many ways they were also similar to those built in earlier days by the local landowners and that proposed by James Stockdale in 1838. They were built from sand, of which there was more than enough nearby, with those sides facing the sea or tides being covered in puddle clay and then limestone. Those sides which would face the recovered land were grassed over. One set of navvies would work ahead building a low embankment or 'toe' several hundred yards long. A second group would follow, concentrating on building the toe up into the embankment proper. As the sand was piled up, the puddlers and masons followed behind to protect the embankment.

It can be seen, therefore, that for each day's work in piling up the sand, the tides, particularly the monthly high tides, would remove much of their handiwork. The contractors resorted to protecting the embankment from the tides with brushwood and stones. In Winster Bay, the river had been flowing such that its channel crossed the course of the railway roughly midway between Blawith Point and Meathop Point. The former river bed, at a lower point than the adjacent sands, formed 'holes' holding around 10 feet of water. In the following March (1855) Burlington was able to walk along the railway embankment to Meathop Fell, now much scarred by the quarrying for limestone and to allow the railway to pass through its tip. He recorded that the pitching and facing was almost complete but the hole where the Winster once flowed was still deep and the weak point on the embankment.

Once completed, William Hanson's men started out across the wider Kent estuary towards the planned location for the Kent viaduct. This was to prove as troublesome, for, whilst the Winster Bay embankment ran from one headland to another, that across the Kent sands was to end mid-estuary. Work started in the summer of 1855 but progress was slow from the start. The embankment was to be breached several times during the course of construction, with men and equipment being rushed from the less troubled work in the Leven estuary to close the breaches. Particularly bad breaches were to occur in October 1855, July 1856 and twice in August 1856. In late November that year there was still 350 yards to go, although work on the 'toe' was complete. Work on the viaduct was already well underway.

To protect this embankment and to keep the Kent flowing under the viaduct, a weir or low embankment was built south from a point near Ulpha on the eastern shore of the Kent estuary, across the point where the embankment would end and the viaduct commence and on for a few hundred yards. Whilst ultimately successful in influencing the course of the river (and later allowing the reclamation of a large tract of land east of Meathop Fell), it couldn't stop the tides from flowing back over the site of the lengthening railway embankment.

On the Leven estuary, work was as slow, but at least there was no Winster Bay to cross. The river Eea (or Cark Beck as it is locally known) was diverted for about 400 yards to avoid the railway passing over it more than once, and all that before it had reached the estuary. Work on the Capeshead embankment, between Cark and the site planned for the Leven viaduct, commenced in April 1853.

No holes are recorded in the sand at Cark Marsh where the embankment crossed the erstwhile course of the beck. Nearby was the road from Cark to Ulverston over the sands. This crossed the course of the railway at Quarry Flat Point. During November 1854 the Lower Holker ratepayers, led

Meathop, looking towards Holme Island and Grange on 25 June 1958. *The quarry here was opened out after circa 1860, the railway having originally passed through a cutting here! Beyond the quarry and the signalbox controlling Meathop sidings is the gasworks erected by the Grange and Cartmel Gas and Water Company. Further on, the line passes over what had been one of the most troublesome sections of the U&LR – the embankment over Winster Bay. The river Winster had once flowed into Morecambe Bay close to Holme Island, but was diverted in 1852 to pass under the railway by a sluice close to the gasworks.*
(CRA Photo Library ref. PEK391)

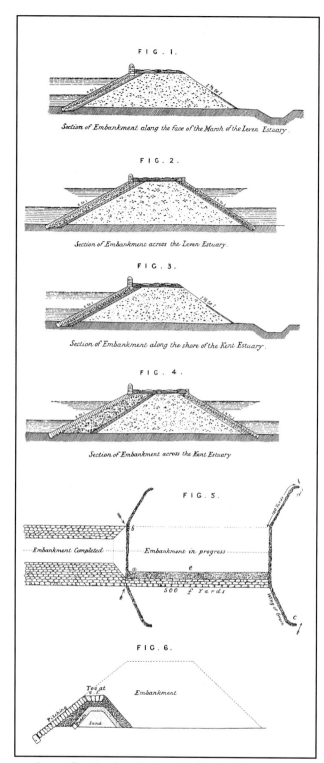

FIG. 1.

Section of Embankment along the face of the Marsh of the Leven Estuary.

FIG. 2.

Section of Embankment across the Leven Estuary.

FIG. 3.

Section of Embankment along the shore of the Kent Estuary.

FIG. 4.

Section of Embankment across the Kent Estuary

FIG. 5.

Embankment Completed ---- *Embankment in progress* ----

500 f Yards

FIG. 6.

Toe at e.f.   Embankment

Pitching   Sand

**James Brunlees' embankments for the Ulverstone &
Lancaster Railway.** *The diagrams indicate the differing
cross-sections of embankment used at various places.
Figures 5 and 6 demonstrate how a low embankment or toe
was built in advance of the main construction across the
river estuaries.*   (From The Engineer)

by James Stockdale and his cousin and fellow landowner Gray Rigge, pushed for a level crossing at Quarry Flat, but Burlington preferred a crossing further east. After some discussions with the Brogdens and Brunlees, the eastern site, close to some new cottages built by the Earl at Crookwheel, was chosen. The Earl was also worried about the drainage of the reclaimed land behind the Capeshead embankment which became part of his Holker estate. This matter would not be quickly settled.

Quarry Flat together with Capes Head and a few points in between were the locations from where limestone was quarried to face the embankments. Sand ramps were built up to embankment level on the landward side to allow the carts to bring up the dressed stone. The remains of one of these can be found west of Quarry Flat, but any others were removed before completion of the railway.

It was April 1855 before the embankment had reached Capes Head. On the 21st of that month James Stelfox started men carting sand for the embankment from there out into the Leven estuary. Within a week he recorded that he was carting clay from nearby Park Head for pitching the embankment. As work on the viaduct was to start that June, extra effort was put to the work on the embankment. This was aided in part by additional horses and carts and in part by the introduction, in late May, of an engine to draw waggons of sand up the bank end. Unfortunately it is not clear whether this was a locomotive or a stationary engine. It took about two weeks work by Henry Brogden (who was a trained locomotive engineer) and Stelfox before it could be coaxed into pulling up more than a waggon or two at a time.

December 1855 saw work on the Capeshead embankment gradually come to a halt. Stelfox recorded that markets were in decline and prices high. What he didn't know was that several banks had called in their loans with the company and Alex Brogden was desperately seeking new sources of funds. Men were discharged and Stelfox closed up the bank end to protect it from the tides. It was protected from the river by a stone weir running from Park Head to the western end of the viaduct. This of course was primarily to divert the river into a permanent channel under the viaduct.

By April 1856 work was again under way and the permanent railway was laid from Cark out past Quarry Flat at least. Stelfox noted an engine passed by that place for the first time on the 21st of that month. By 28 April Stelfox resumed work on the embankment beyond Capeshead point, with nineteen horses and carts at work. On 10 May another attempt to speed up work was tried when Henry Brogden introduced some novel method of loading sand into the wagons. A month later Stelfox estimated the bank was being lengthened by about 8 yards per day. Work on pitching the embankment was under way again about a month later.

On 2 July rails had been delivered to the bank end by the Brogden's flat *Calder*. The Capeshead embankment was 270 yards short of its target by 9 July 1856, although the toe was extended that far. During August 1856 Stelfox first mentioned problems with a hole at the bank end. It would be well into October before the problem was solved and work could continue towards the viaduct end. It was effectively completed by 20 January. Within the following few weeks the incline at Capeshead Point was pulled up and the quarry at Quarry Flat was closed and given up.

The Capeshead embankment was not officially completed until 7 March 1857, when Mrs Alexander Brogden 'laid' the last pitching stone and unveiled a plaque to commemorate the event. James Stelfox presented a commemorative mell or mallet on behalf of the workmen to mark the occasion. Directors and other important personalities were there, along with the navvies. No doubt the Galloways' men also observed the festivity. Alex and Henry Brogden made speeches, as did James Ramsden. Refreshments were passed around and a brass band played.

As the embankment was completed, Burlington was still frustrated by the lack of activity on the drainage of his reclaimed lands. In April 1857 work was finally started to block the reclaimed land from the sea, there being a gap of about 100 ft. between Capeshead Point and the nearby embankment which could let the tides through. The gap was blocked by an embankment somewhat lower than the railway embankment but sufficient to do its job. A drain was then dug along the inside of the railway embankment back towards Quarry Flat. A similar drain was needed in Cark Marsh, this leading into a stream already crossed by the embankment where sea doors were provided to stop flooding. Sea doors also protected the drain at Capes Head, where water was let off for the first time on 21 April. Things never being easy in the U&LR embankments, the short embankment at Capes Head was breached by the tide on 24 April. Although fixed the following day, Burlington was not impressed. In September the drain was still incomplete, as he was to remind one of the Brogdens. The Brogdens were, however, not too keen to proceed. It was to be over a year later when Sir Joseph Paxton, as arbitrator in the event of a dispute, inspected the drainage with Devonshire's agent, Drewry. Paxton had words with Alex Brogden and the matter seems to have been successfully resolved.

McClean and Stileman had originally planned to cross the Leven and Kent on 737-yard-long wooden viaducts, each with a 30 ft. opening bridge and wide enough for a single line. Plans were prepared to this effect by them in 1852 and submitted for Admiralty approval. McClean & Stileman then resigned as Engineers in February 1853. The new Engineer, Brunlees, recommended iron be used for the viaducts rather than wood. A national shortage of timber following the unrest with Russia may have also influenced things. The Directors reported this change to their shareholders in February 1855, when the company was ready to start work on the viaducts. The Leven had been brought under some control with the building of stone weirs to move its course to the viaduct site (and protect the sea embankments), with similar weirs on the Kent, the Greenodd tradesmen having agreed to this.

The company records for the period are scant at best so we are uncertain who tendered for the Leven viaduct. What we do know is that on 28 March 1855 Brunlees was showing one of the Galloway brothers the proposed site of the Leven viaduct. On 2 April Mr Allen started work building the abutment from which the viaduct would head out at Tredley Point, with Mr Pattinson getting the necessary limestone. Two days later James Stelfox learned that the viaduct contract was let to W & J Galloway, noted builders of boilers and constructional ironwork of Knott Mill, Manchester. At the end of April the Galloways placed an order for the ironwork – with John Brogden & Sons' newly purchased ironworks at Tondu, Glamorgan! This was to prove a troublesome subcontract.

John Galloway and a gang of men arrived in Ulverston on 1 May 1855 and set up an ironworks (strictly a foundry) on the west bank of Ulverston Canal. By mid-June they were driving their first piles into the sands of the Leven estuary at Tredley. These early piles had proper foundations on firm bedrock. The abutment collapsed in mid July whilst Galloway's men were driving a trial pile.

Brunlees and Galloway had failed to find a hard bed under the sands once they were away from Tredley Point. A series of experiments then took place with trial piles being sunk. This was a slow process of trial and error but by March the trials were over, the method perfected and permanent piles were sunk.

In August 1856 Galloways were preparing the components of the drawbridge, although it seems the Tondu works were having difficulty making parts to Galloways' specification. They notified the company that the contract would be delayed if their requirements weren't met.

Leven Viaduct, July 1857. *A test train of U&LR ore wagons, hauled by one of John Brogden & Sons' locomotives stands on the sliding bridge, possibly the first train to cross the viaduct. The locomotive is believed to be the former East Lancashire Railway 0-4-2 Scarborough. The gentleman in the tall hat is believed to be John Galloway, whose firm built the viaduct.*

(Collection of Peter Robinson)

All the same progress was being made, and the westernmost piers in the tip of the Capeshead embankment were finally put in place on 2 February 1857. The first set of girders had been put in place on the Leven viaduct on 25 November 1856. It may have been that progress needed to be seen, as less than two weeks later Burlington was inspecting the line with John Brogden, Ramsden, Brunlees and McClean. This was in preparation for the Furness Railway's loan to see the U&LR completed.

On 23 February 1857, W & J Galloway were confident they would have the viaduct in a state ready to lay the longitudinal timbers and rails on 1 May. However, fate struck again. During the driving of the piles across the Leven estuary, there appears to have been no serious problems with the shipping heading up to Greenodd and Roudsea wharves. However, as soon as the girders were across the viaduct and with the opening span being erected, the 'flat' (or schooner) *Sarah Jane* sailed into the viaduct and broke four columns! Brunlees showed the damage to John Brogden on May Day and the ships owner, Thompson, was sued for damages. Thompson settled out of court on 30 July for £45 plus costs. Another vessel ran into the viaduct on 24 July, breaking a column. This was badly timed as it delayed the company from inviting the Board of Trade to inspect the line.

To a certain extent the railway company can only blame themselves for not putting measures in place to reduce the risk. Whilst they had agreed with the Admiralty that the viaduct and opening span should be protected by fenders, these were not put up until after the viaduct was complete.

On 22nd May, Brogden's vessel *Calder* was loaded with rails and chairs for the viaduct. The permanent road was laid across the viaduct between 1 and 6 July. The following week Burlington observed that it was in an advanced state, and didn't appear surprised that the company planned to open the line in early August. The first locomotive, Brogden's construction locomotive *Scarborough* ran over the viaduct on 18 July with Stelfox on the footplate. It is probably this event that John Galloway had photographed.

In parallel to all this work was the building of the Kent viaduct. Tenders for this were not invited until the end of July 1856 when the problems in crossing the Leven had been sorted out. The tenders from eleven firms were opened at the board meeting on 5 August. Galloways' was almost the lowest tender, beaten by £30 at £13,470 by Messrs Featherstone of Manchester. One tender had not been opened, Messrs Kennard having sent it to the company's Ulverston office rather than Brogden's office in Manchester. Featherstone must have got wind of the missing tender as they submitted a second tender the following day in time for the decision by the board. Kennard had offered to build the Kent viaduct for £12,400; Featherstone undercut him by £400! Discussions were held between the Directors, Galloway and Featherstone. The board were not happy with the people named as sureties by Featherstone and he was given until the 19th to satisfy them. The tender was finally accepted on 19 August, Featherstone's sureties being John Morley and Messrs J W and J Chandler.

Morley had been with Featherstone at Fighting Cocks (Arnside) on 12 August looking for a site for their workshops and ironworks. On the same day that the tender was formally accepted, Featherstone began building his workshops. He was soon busy sinking piles, with six in by 27 October. On 21 November Burlington observed that they were 'getting in fast drawing piles for the viaduct over the Kent'. By December the weir between the piers was being laid.

Whilst work progressed on the viaduct, there was the small matter of the opening span. The design for this was somewhat more advanced than that built on the Leven viaduct. Instead of the moveable decking having wheels which ran on rails, the deck girders themselves acted as the rails and rolled down wheels attached to the main viaduct structure.

As far as the railway company was concerned there was little traffic to the ancient port of Milnthorpe, especially since the Lancaster Canal's northern extension had reached Kendal and the Lancaster & Carlisle and Kendal & Windermere railways had opened. There was no need for the agreed opening span here and, even if it was built, they had no plans to make it operational. They had not considered the Kendal Chamber of Commerce!

The Kendal tradesmen commissioned a civil engineer named Ure and on 9 April 1857 accompanied him on a walk down the Kent from Levens Bridge (the lowest bridging point) to Arnside to see if it would be feasible to make the river navigable up to Levens Bridge. The U&LR called upon their new ally, the Earl of Burlington, to get the Admiralty decision reversed. Burlington agreed it was 'quite uncalled for' and promised to write to Sir Charles Wood of the Admiralty regarding the matter.

Holme Island. *First built as a hunting lodge in the 1830s, the house and island was acquired by John Brogden around 1856. The family moved here from Lightburn at Ulverston around 1857, and were resident until the early 1880s when their fortunes collapsed spectacularly. In U&LR days the railway was effectively run from here. James Brunlees had his office here at the time of the line's opening. (Courtesy Grange over Sands Photographic Society)*

An Admiralty enquiry followed on 18 April at the Cross Keys in Milnthorpe, under J G C Curtis CE where the necessary evidence from both parties was heard. Whilst Curtis and the Admiralty deliberated, the Mayor of Kendal, J Whitwell, called a meeting of the local manufacturers and tradesmen to protest against the railway company's proposals. Whitwell had heard that the Admiralty were keen to see the navigation preserved. This is curious as in the following month the U&LR requested permission from the Admiralty to complete the viaduct without an opening section (which, in fact, they did). The Admiralty's initial response during that summer was to agree with the company but advising that they retained the power to request the opening be made available.

In December 1857, possibly after further representations from Kendal, the Admiralty gave notice to provide the opening. The company disputed this, based on their interpretation of the earlier agreements (and the fact that it would involve rebuilding those spans of the viaduct). The Admiralty insisted. Featherstone was invited to tender for the necessary work: in February 1858 he estimated he could do the work for £523.

Negotiations were to continue through 1858. A petition was made for a station at Arnside, to which the railway agreed. A siding at Arnside was authorised in May 1858 and a basic passenger station was agreed in November 1858. The Admiralty acquiesced to the company's demand and withdrew their notice for the opening section. The Kendal Chamber of Commerce persisted with their demands, however. In February 1859 they would withdraw their objections provided that the railway company erected a wharf at Arnside together with a road along the shore from Arnside to Sandside. This was done, the road running from a level crossing at Arnside station. The conditions were met, and negotiations closed in July 1860. All was confirmed by an Admiralty enquiry on 7 August 1861. The pier, of course, still stands although the road was replaced during the construction of the FR's Hincaster branch line in the 1870s.

It was to be 4 July 1857 before Stelfox received orders from Alex Brogden to lay the permanent road across the Kent Viaduct. The necessary materials were shipped across from Canal Foot at Ulverston. The work was soon complete and on 15 July the first engine was run through Grange. Three days later Stelfox noted that a train of seven trucks came over the Kent Viaduct loaded with Alex Brogden's furniture for his new abode on Holme Island.

Work on the two contracts between Blawith Point and Cark didn't commence until 2 June 1856 when contractor William Eckersley started work on the Kirkhead cutting, on the Wyke – Blawith Point contract. From this cutting through limestone he could obtain the necessary facing stone for the sea embankment. On 18 October 1856 Burlington walked along the line of railway from Grange to Wyke. He noted that 'a good deal of work has now been done and many hands are employed'. Although the line was a relatively easy construction compared with the embankments out in the Kent and Leven estuaries, weaving along the foreshore the work was not without incident. On 5 November 1856 a slip occurred at Kirkhead and on 20 February 1857 a serious accident occurred to two men at Grange, when they had   prepared a blast which failed to fire. The men returned and started boring again, causing the original blast to explode. William Mitchell, 49, of Lindale lost his sight in both eyes and the blast blew off his trousers. The other, James Holmes, who lived at the navvies' huts, was lucky to escape with less injury. It would be June 1857 before the finishing touches to the track were completed.

John Brogden & Sons retained the Cark to Wyke contract. This included the deep cutting south of Cark village together with another east of Flookburgh village from which much of the low embankments on the section could be built. In early November Stelfox began excavating the Flookburgh cutting. December saw frosts and snow on the Cartmel peninsula and on the 1st of that month work was stopped by Brogden's supervisor, Bell. Work was still at a standstill

on the 3rd when Alex Brogden took Bell off the works for neglecting them, and diarist James Stelfox was instructed to take charge. Work was got under way again in the Flookburgh cutting. This work was let to Scott's and Lloyd's gangs at a rate of 4d per yard, who were to take the spoil and tip it to take the embankment eastward towards Wyke. They received 2d per yard for soil moved.

In digging the cutting the men found traces of iron ore. In July 1857 the Ulverston Advertiser carried an advertisement for John Helme, owner of the adjacent land, offering permits to search for ore. Various companies were to drill bore holes in the fields behind Cark station in the coming years, but no commercial mining took place.

By March 1857 the embankment extended to Wraysholme where the embankment was formed by side cutting. However on 13 March, the cutting at Flookburgh began to slip and in April the embankment beyond Flookburgh was sinking. Work on filling the 'station field' at Cark, which included much wet ground and a seasonal pond, started in April and didn't finish until three months later. At its eastern end, the embankment beyond the occupation overbridge at Wyke was not under way until 16 June 1857. This was quickly completed, as track had already been laid from Cark out to the bridge. Stelfox took a locomotive out from Flookburgh on 15 June.

Some consideration had been made for the Canal – Tridley Point section to be offered to Boulton, as an extension of his existing U&LR contract during 1851. However it would be 26 December 1855 before Messrs Bell and Kerr, Brogden's supervisors, started the men to work at Next Ness; the work was carried out by Brogden's own men. At the end of March 1856 the western section towards the canal viaduct was under way. Rather than using materials from the Pennington cutting, as originally considered, the embankment from the canal viaduct to Next Ness was built by side cutting, a technique involving digging earth from either side of the new embankment. This was to prove troublesome.

On 14 April 1856 work was started eastward from Next Ness bridge but it was to be 3 November before Stelfox started carting sand to form the embankment out to Tredley Point. This work continued through the frost and snows of that December. From 6 December an engine was assisting with the work here. Despite some damage in a storm on the night of 8 December, the bank was completed by the 20th.

In April 1857 Stelfox thought that the Next Ness embankment was more stable. Work continued, marred by the death of a 14-year-old lad that month: he had been involved in emptying the waggons at the tip end and had climbed on the next-to-last waggon to ride back to the excavation site. The train started with a jolt and young Ardacre fell, to be crushed by the last waggon. The embankment was slipping again on 17 June 1857. On 23 July the push was on to complete the embankment. The line was complete and permanent road laid from Carnforth through to Plumpton, but the two tips at Next Ness embankment had still not been joined. From the previous day the Furness were bringing loads of dirt from a spoil bank at Pennington to get the work completed. On 30 July the embankment was still slipping and was being cited for the delay to the opening of the line. When the line was inspected on 7 August 1857 with a view to opening, the government inspector noted the signs of recent slipping in his list of defects.

The last sections of line to be built were between the junction of the Lancaster & Carlisle Railway at Carnforth, and the eastern end of the Kent Viaduct at Arnside. The section from Carnforth to Arnside was let to William Eckersley whilst the embankment out to the Kent Viaduct was constructed by Brogden's men. The Lancaster & Carlisle railway carried out alterations at Carnforth station. Although Eckersley's men started some work at Carnforth in August 1855; their target was to complete the line by summer 1856 but, officially, there were difficulties getting

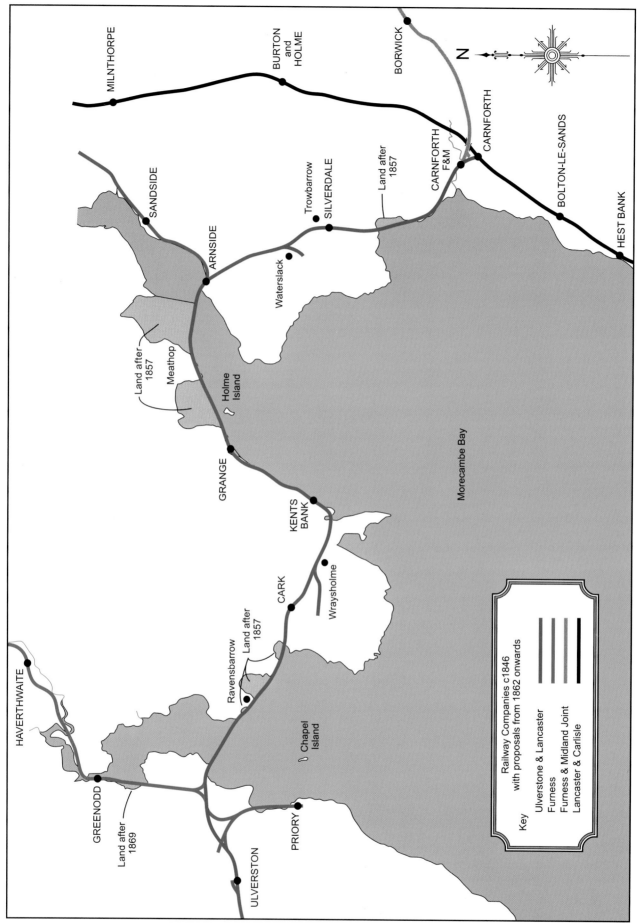

The route of the Ulverstone & Lancaster Railway. *As can be seen, a practical route overtook the need for land reclamation, which became a far remove from the visions of earlier railway promoters.*
(Drawing by Alan Johnstone)

the land and problems borrowing money. It was January 1857 when equipment, freed up from the earlier works, was sent to Arnside to put the finishing touches to the Carnforth section. In a piece of Directorial 'spin', the report to shareholders at the end of February 1857 claimed that it had been ready for several months and used to transport materials for the Kent Viaduct. Even after opening there were shortcomings in this section of line. On 16 November 1857 Stelfox complained at the unfinished state of the ballasting and permanent road.

At the end of July 1857, the Engineer and Directors of the U&LR were ready to open their railway and the Board of Trade were notified. Arrangements had been made with the FR for them to run the trains and with the Lancaster & Carlisle railway for trains to run through to Lancaster. Advertisements for the opening of the railway to the public on 10 August were placed in the local newspapers.

Lt Col. Yolland inspected the line on 7 August 1857 and duly made his report to his masters. All was not well. Seven items were specifically mentioned as requiring attention, including concerns with points and signals, the lack of station buildings at Kents Bank, the absence of lodges at the level crossings, the slip on the embankment at Next Ness, the need to complete the passing siding at Cark and its platform, and various items on the viaducts. However it was the presence of three apparently unauthorised level crossings that caused consternation for Captain Galton back at the Board of Trade. The line was not approved for opening for passenger trains. The Goods and Mineral trains started running, as advertised, on the 10th.

Brunlees set to remedy the defects with the construction of the line whilst correspondence was entered into with the Board of Trade regarding the crossings. These were at Plumpton, Holme Island and near Arnside (Black Dyke crossing). Brunlees admitted to having misled Yolland regarding the Plumpton crossing: it was not a public road but an occupation crossing for Plumpton Hall farm, recently occupied by the Brogdens. The crossing at Holme Island replaced an authorised crossing a few hundred yards further east to allow an old road over Winster Bay to cross the line of the railway. It had seemingly been little used. The only unauthorised crossing was in fact that at Black Dyke, where the line had apparently deviated from the planned line (but

within agreed limits). A planned bridge for the Arnside to Beetham road was not now feasible and the company substituted the crossing, with the agreement of the affected landowners.

Despite the Board of Trade being still annoyed about the crossings (bureaucracy over practicality – still a Civil Service trait!), on 18 August, they instructed Yolland to return to Carnforth. He inspected the line again on the 22nd and agreed to its opening. The Board were duly informed and arranged their opening ceremonies for 26 August.

The opening was carried out in grand style. The stations and viaducts were decorated with flags, bunting and banners over the line celebrating the railway, the viaducts and the Brogdens! A special train of dignitaries ran from Ulverston to Carnforth. Here the great and good from all over Lancashire, together with Burlington's sister and family (her husband being an FR Director!) joined the train for the journey to Furness Abbey. Here a grand marquee was erected and Mrs Slaney provided the inevitable feast. Toasts and speeches were made. The last link had been made!

Alexander Brogden and some of his fellow Directors entertained the workmen at Lightburn on the following day. After thanking them for their hard work, the Wesleyan Managing Director of the Ulverstone & Lancaster Railway reminded his men of the benefits of sobriety!

Given the delays, the line wasn't opened to passenger traffic officially until the beginning of the September timetable. The coaches between Ulverston and Lancaster across the bay stopped at the same time. Burlington noted that the trains weren't very punctual. Traffic didn't immediately come up to expectations either. The opening coincided with the inevitable slackening in trade; also the majority of Furness ore was still being transported by sea and only a token amount heading by rail to South Staffordshire, although that was soon to change.

As was described, construction of the sea embankments was more difficult and took longer than expected. It should also be noted that the Crimean War occurred during a long period of the construction (1854-6) when prices of food and timber rose. With the extra pay to be found together with the cost of iron for the viaducts (more expensive than the wood construction originally proposed and the official reason

Arnside. *A view of Black Dyke Level Crossing looking towards Silverdale in the 1930s. This level crossing caused some consternation at the Board of Trade in 1857 when, during the official inspection to open the line, it was realised that a bridge had been authorised at this point. In true civil-service fashion, the mandarins of Whitehall wouldn't let the matter rest, even when the line was authorised to be opened to passenger traffic. The situation was rectified in the U&LR Act 1858.* (CRA Photo Library ref. PA0023)

Opening day! *The Kent Viaduct was bedecked with flags and banners to celebrate the opening of the U&LR. The artist of the* Illustrated London News *has depicted the first train heading towards Carnforth, from where it would return westwards as the official opening train, with the Brogdens and their guests, to Furness Abbey for a celebratory Dinner.*

(From The Illustrated London News*)*

for the extra costs), the funds the company could raise as shares or through loans proved insufficient. By 1856 lenders proved hard to find. In February Alex Brogden reported to his Board that he had been going around the London insurance offices trying to borrow money in return for Debentures, but with no success. Payments for land and securities began to be made in Debentures. In July the company managed to borrow £10,000 for Debentures with the London Joint Stock Bank. A month later the FR Board were aware that the U&LR needed £30,000 to complete their line. In fact the company went back to the London Joint Stock Bank, who insisted that the existing £10,000 loan be paid off before lending the company the £25,750 it actually needed. The unexpected demand for extra money was satisfied by a loan of £10,000 from James Garstang. From around that time loans were obtained in return for 5 year Debentures, rather than the previous 3 year loans.

Whilst this would tide them over for a few months things began to get serious. Events in the Pennines were also to influence events. In October 1856 Burlington noted that a meeting had been held in Kirkby Lonsdale to promote the South Durham & Lancashire Union Railway. This would provide an outlet for Furness haematite to the ironworks of Middlesbrough and County Durham. The Ulverstone & Lancaster Railway was no longer just a useful scheme but one that would actually be advantageous to the Furness Company: it must be completed! At the U&LR Directors meeting on 13 December, the Brogdens noted that they had been offered a loan of £50,000 by the FR Board. The loan was made in equal halves by Lords Burlington and Buccleuch in return for £150,000 of non-voting shares, to be split between the noble benefactors. The Furness indemnified their Lordships and insisted on Stephen Eddy becoming a Director of the U&LR. The loan, for five years, in line with the existing U&LR Debenture policy, was to be from 1 June 1857. In return the Brogdens had to put up £20,000 in proportion to the money borrowed from Burlington and Buccleuch.

The agreement was ratified by the U&LR Shareholders on 27 January 1857 and Mr Eddy was duly elected a Director. At a Board meeting on the same day, a curious

anomaly was resolved. The Board noted that land had been bought under the terms of the 1851 U&LR Act but conveyance had in fact been made to John Brogden. He was now to be charged for this, and land from the Lightburn and Seawood estates (at Ulverston and Kents Bank) were to be conveyed to the Company.

Things were not totally satisfactory with the banks. On 10 August 1857, Garstang again bailed out the company by taking out £5000 worth of Debentures in lieu of ones to the London Joint Stock Bank.

One of the points in the 1856 agreement with the Furness was that, if necessary, the U&LR would go to Parliament for authority to raise further capital, primarily to cover them for when they got around to doubling the line. By November 1857 it would appear that the U&LR would not only need £72,000 to double their line but had also over-extended themselves by £78,000! They submitted a Bill to Parliament to raise the £150,000 plus £50,000 in Debentures. In evidence it was submitted that the sea embankments had needed to be raised by 4 feet, as well as having been built for double line, resulting in £70,000 extra cost. The cost of building iron viaducts instead of wooden ones caused £15,000 of additional costs. The company had also spent between £5,000 and £6,000 on enlarging Carnforth station, not including the cost of land.

The Bill included sanction for Black Dyke level crossing and to allow the potential sale or lease of the company to the Furness. The Bill also sought authority for the FR to raise capital to buy the U&LR. An interesting point in what became the Ulverstone & Lancaster Railway Act 1858 was what could happen to the property owned by the company. The FR were authorised to buy whole or part of the railway, works, lands, property and effects. If the transfer was of the railway but not the lands reclaimed under the 1851 Act, then the U&LR would become the Ulverstone Lands Company!

The U&LR 1858 Act received Royal Assent on 12 July 1858. That November Burlington noted that the Company were looking to the Furness for £100,000. The FR Board offered this sum on condition that the U&LR was sold to them in return for 4% Preference shares. Alex Brogden,

The Railway at Kents Bank. *A sketch from the mid 1860s, following the doubling of the railway and erection of the station house. The novelty of the new railway was not lost on visitors and, from the number of people apparently walking along the railway, locals too! At left can be seen Abbot Hall. Between it and the railway station stands the original Kents Bank Hotel. Already villas are appearing, spurred by the arrival of the railway,* (Author's Collection).

who presumably was sitting outside the meeting room, rejected the offer. Much to Burlington's chagrin that was not the end of the matter: FR Solicitor Currey carried on negotiations with the Brogdens right up to 17 December, when the idea was abandoned.

After all of these financial difficulties, by the end of 1858 the company could afford to pay a 1.5% dividend. Dividends rose through the coming years until they reached a respectable 5% for the second half of 1860.

Whilst the company was sorting out its finances it did have difficulties making final payments for the construction of the line. Galloways were still demanding payment in January 1858 whilst during that February even Engineer Brunlees had to threaten the company to get his remuneration. At the same time some thought was given to expansion. During early 1858 Brunlees had surveyed a line to Newby Bridge for the company and in December that year the prospect of a L&CR branch from Hest Bank to Morecambe turned the Directors' thoughts to a possible line from Carnforth to Hornby on the North Western Railway. Nothing came of either scheme, although the merchants and tradesmen of Greenodd were to hear about the Newby Bridge scheme in 1860 and made sure it was reported in the Ulverston Advertiser!

In January 1858 Messrs Schneider and Hannay began negotiations for an ironworks on land at Hindpool, north of Barrow. The first two of three furnaces were blown in on 17 October 1859. This occasion gave the U&LR extra traffic in the form of coke, initially from the Wigan area and, after the opening of the SDLUR in July 1861, from County Durham. At the same time the iron trade was recovering such that in 1859 69,028 tons of Furness ore were being delivered to South Staffordshire ironworks by rail over U&LR plus another 3,777 tons from West Cumberland. Brogden had the benefit of an additional 6,722 tons going out through

the Ulverston Canal. All this traffic put a strain on the single line U&LR and a phased doubling was planned. The first section, from Ulverston down to the Leven Viaduct, was completed by August 1860 with the section from the single line viaduct through to Cark being inspected on 30 July 1861.

With the opening of the SDLUR, the Furness Railway Directors wanted full control of the line from Carnforth through to Barrow ironworks. At the same time, although traffic was now increasing, the U&LR had not raised all the capital needed for doubling the line. Additionally their 1856 debentures would be coming to term and need either repaying or renegotiating. At a Board meeting on 31 October 1861, the U&LR Directors considered a lease to the FR for 6% preference shares. Ramsden, for the Furness, and Alex Brogden, for the U&LR, negotiated and on 13 November 1861 they agreed to a lease for 2 years at 5%, then 1000 years at 6%. The FR Directors were more bullish, and instead offered to purchase the U&LR outright at 6% from 1 January 1862, under the terms of the 1858 Act, for a sum of £427,939 14s 4d (for which £298,000 worth of special 6% preference shares were issued). It should be noted that the 1858 Act effectively extended the U&LR shareholding and borrowings to a potential £493,333 6s 8d. That had obviously not been achieved. The Furness also purchased the Ulverston Canal Navigation Co. outright from the Brogdens for £22,004 15s 0d, thus relieving the Brogden family of any control in local transport. The deal was ratified by U&LR and FR shareholders on 21 January 1862.

Much of what happened after the purchase of the U&LR is well embedded in Furness Railway history. Some general facts pertaining to the Ulverston to Carnforth section are worth noting for thoroughness. These are covered in the following chapters.

Approaching Wraysholme crossing from Cark. *Ex LMS 4F 0-6-0 No. 44454 approaches the Wraysholme Up Distant signal with the 11-05 am Ulverston to Carnforth trip working on 10 July 1956. The Wraysholme distant is one of several signals installed in 1917 in connection with the Airship Factory siding. Forty years on the top of the signal post is showing signs of deterioration, with large pieces of concrete having fallen away, exposing the reinforcement wires.* (CRA Photo Library ref. PEJ468)

Cark. *Ex-FR 3F 0-6-0 No. 52509 prepares to shunt a wagon carrying agricultural machinery from the 12-05 pm Carnforth to Ulverston goods train on 10 July 1956. The train is standing on the down line in front of the signal box. The tracks in the foreground are a pair of lay-by sidings, which were used, among other things, to hold excursion trains to Cark on Cartmel Race days.*
(CRA Photo Library ref. PEJ488)

Industrial Development

4

Meathop, looking north-east along the Meathop embankment on 25 June 1958. *The short siding serving the gasworks of the Grange & Cartmel Gas and Water Company is on the left, with Meathop sidings and signalbox under Meathop Fell beyond. The cottages below and to the left of the embankment belonged to the gasworks, but were architecturally similar to the Level Crossing cottages found along the Ulverston and Lancaster line.* (CRA Photo Library ref. PEK387)

WHEN THE ULVERSTON & Lancaster Railway opened there was little industry immediately close to the line, excepting, of course, agriculture. It is ironic that of all the railway schemes for crossing Morecambe Bay, whilst the inland schemes passed the mills and ironworks of the Leven Valley, and the cross-bay schemes were to reclaim thousands of acres of land to be sold at a profit, the U&LR was least blessed. It neither served any industries nor sold significant acreages to pay for construction of the line (any land reclaimed was sold at cost to John Brogden or to the neighbouring landowners).

Whilst local agriculture went through the national peaks and troughs, a couple of aspects are worthy of note. From before the opening of the railway, Furness life centred around the weekly market at Ulverston. Each Thursday special trains and tickets were available for many years from stations in the district and special arrangements had to be made at Cark and Grange for the additional shunting of cattle wagons. As noted elsewhere, cattle sales commenced at Cark in 1858 and in later years the great and the good from across the country would arrive at Cark en route for prize livestock sales at Holker Hall.

Another significant but now forgotten aspect of country life was the horse. Horse breeding was carried out by farmers throughout the region. Many rivalries came to the fore at the local agricultural shows when their horses were shown in competition! In the early 20th century horses were bred by the Dickinson family, millers at Cark. Whilst many went for use by constabularies and such like, many showed their form on the racecourse!

Now back to industry. Ulverston, of course, had its mills and manufactures, but at the other end of the line Carnforth was a small roadside village. Within a few years, however,

activity was under way to exploit the mineral wealth of the district, from extraction through to manufacture. The major industry, more by geographical chance than by design, was to be the quarrying of limestone. Searches were made for seams of haematite ore close to the line but nothing was found to match the extent of the seams in Furness or West Cumberland. In the twentieth century, war and the prospect of a new era in aviation almost brought a further industry to the area. Industries were also created to service the growing towns and villages.

As noted earlier, substantial amounts of limestone were used to face the sea embankments between Arnside and Plumpton. This was obtained from small quarries or from the cuttings at Kirkhead, near Kents Bank, and Meathop. With the opening of the modern ironworks in the area, first at Barrow, followed in swift succession by works at Carnforth and Askam and then finally at Ulverston (North Lonsdale), there was a massive demand for limestone as flux for the blast furnaces.

The cutting at Meathop was an odd affair, passing through the headland close to its tip. It was an obvious choice for a quarry, allowing limestone to be taken first from the seaward side of the cutting, thus opening it out, and later on the inland side. As early as October 1860 a builder from Barrow was hiring quarrymen to work at Meathop.

In 1868 Grange Gasworks was built down by the river Winster, below the headland and railway. The gasworks were served by a short siding from the Up line and from 1873 controlled by one of the new signal boxes installed along the U&L line in that year. The location of the signal box indicates the extent of the quarrying. By that time sufficient limestone had been removed to both open out the cutting and allow a further Up siding to be in place. Thus

***Trowbarrow Limeworks,
Silverdale, circa 1900.***
*The works of Northern
Quarries Limited were
connected to Trowbarrow
Quarry, off the photograph
to the right, by a narrow
gauge incline. Several
Northern Quarries wagons
stand with one from the
Midland Railway on the
sidings, which extended
from Silverdale station.
(CRA Photo Library
ref. WAI056)*

the limestone could be loaded from the west side of the line. The 1877 FR working timetable indicates a daily goods train stopping at Meathop to shunt for limestone traffic but a later one of 1882 shows no such workings. Presumably the quarry had closed by that time. The Up siding became a lay-by siding, supplemented by a Down siding in 1884. Quarrying seems to have been carried out intermittently thereafter. In 1903 the FR Board authorized a new siding into the quarry, suggesting some activity.

Trowbarrow quarry and lime works lay to the north of Silverdale station. The quarry was about a third of a mile from the railway, with the lime kilns being erected alongside the line. Connection was via an inclined plane railway. Trowbarrow was developed by James Ward, who leased the land from the Leighton Hall estate from about 1870. Ward, a native of the Fylde, appears to have served an apprenticeship as a builder in Barrow, but at the age of 21 branched out into quarrying limestone. He built a Hoffman continuous limekiln alongside the railway, producing lime for agricultural use and for cement. Much stone was also sent to the growing number of ironworks in the area.

Ward's business grew, with the setting up of further quarries at Sandside, on the Dallam Tower estate, and in Leicestershire. The output from Sandside also passed along the U&L section. Although Sandside was on the Hincaster branch, its goods yard and the quarry were served by trip workings along the U&L line.

In the 1890s Ward was looking for further markets for his products. To allow for the financing of a paving plant at Trowbarrow, among other things, Ward set up the Northern Quarries Company in 1898 to take over his businesses. His experiments into using limestone for road and other surfaces bore fruit with the first of a number of patents involving tar-coated limestone, that for Quarrite, in 1900. Its first major application was in Blackpool three years later. It should be noted that E P Hooley didn't patent tarmacadam (tar-coated slag) as a road surface until 1902. The Quarrite works included a tar distillation and blending plant (using coal tar from local gasworks) and mixing plants. The finished product was shipped by rail in distinctive wagons owned by the company. It was this plant, in January 1908, that suffered a major fire, resulting in the calling out of fire engines from Carnforth and Lancaster as well as the FR's own rail fire engine, powered by 2-4-0 loco No. 1. The Up line between Arnside and Silverdale was closed until the fire was out.

Northern Quarries widened its surface product range but still a significant proportion of its output was limestone for ironworks, being shipped as far afield as Middlesbrough and Scotland. However, with the onset of the Great War, the demand for road materials plummeted and Northern

Quarries suffered: it was wound up in 1916. Four years later Ward set up New Northern Quarries as a limited company to run his empire. By the mid-1920s, road building was on the increase again. A Quarrite plant was set up in 1925 at nearby Sandside quarry to meet demand. From 1930 Trowbarrow's road products were being transported by road (whilst Sandside continued to ship Quarrite by rail), leaving the limestone traffic on rail. New Northern Quarries closed Trowbarrow quarry in 1959, with the mixing plant using limestone from nearby quarries until it too was closed in 1970. The rival Tarmac Company had taken over New Northern Quarries in 1964. The sidings for New Northern Quarries were retained until Silverdale goods yard formally closed in March 1964.

Waterslack (or Middlebarrow) quarry, between Silverdale and Arnside, appears to have also been opened out around 1870. In December 1871 a pointsman was appointed to Waterslack by the FR. The trailing siding was put in from the Down line, adjacent to an occupation crossing giving access to the site. During 1886 signals were installed to protect the siding, controlled from a new ground frame. In 1915 the ground frame was moved into a simple raised cabin. The cabin lasted until 1954 when formal signalling was removed. Quarrying continued into the 1990s. Rail traffic had ceased, however, during the 1970s, when BR stopped buying ballast there and the siding was finally removed in 1978.

From the beginning, the Ulverstone & Lancaster Company must have realised that the climb from the Leven Viaduct up to Ulverston and on to Lindal would be a challenge to their trains. This is especially so given that, on the Furness lines until 1866, all trains were hauled by either Bury-type 0-4-0s or (from 1852) by tiny Fairbairn 2-2-2WTs. Whilst these became increasingly larger with each new delivery, they were still small engines. When it is considered that, even by 1899, the Furness limited its smaller locos (including the 0-6-0s of 1866) to no more than 16 loaded mineral or pig iron wagons (including brake van), 24 merchandise wagons or 32 empties unaided on this section, what chance had the 0-4-0s? Either the trains were short, two locomotives were used, or the trains were split and hauled in sections.

In 1867 a pair of dedicated banking locomotives were purchased by the FR. These were 0-6-0 tank locomotives with extended side tanks specifically for pushing goods and mineral trains up to Lindal. In May 1869, Col. Hutchinson, the Board of Trade Inspector, reported that there was a pair of sidings on the Down side at the then new Plumpton Junction. When these had been installed is not known but their purpose was to allow trains to be split when the bank

Waterslack Quarry. *A group of quarrymen pose for the camera during a break, with an assortment of LMS and, surprisingly, a Great Western Railway wagon in the siding. (CRA Photo Library ref. WAI054)*

engines were not available. Even in 1877 the sidings were referred to as Leven Sidings, although the junction and signal box were referred to as Plumpton Junction. This suggests that the sidings predated the Lakeside branch.

There is the possibility of a further siding, off the southerly of the Leven sidings into the Plumpton Hall estate. In 1861 the Plumpton Mining Company announced that it had found indications of a seam of haematite. Before 1873 the Furness Iron & Steel Company were mining haematite in the old workings. In 1882 the mineral lease was held by its successor, the Askam & Mouzell company. The ore won would be taken to the Askam ironworks. Similar exploration was under way at Cark during this period. Signs of haematite had been found during excavation of the Flookburgh cutting. In April 1861 the Cumberland company were said to have found evidence of a workable seam in a field close to the station. The announcement was premature and no mine was sunk. Others were to try, again with no success.

The sidings, together with the junction of the Lakeside branch facing Ulverston, were controlled from Plumpton Junction signal box, located on the south side of the line at the point of the junction. Further east, beyond Plumpton Crossing, Leven Junction signal box controlled the east-facing junction onto the branch. The two arms of the Lakeside branch met at Greenodd Junction, before heading north to Greenodd. Traffic on the branch commenced at the end of March 1869, when goods trains started running as far as Greenodd. The branch opened throughout in June that year, although it would be September before the station at Haverthwaite was opened. Whilst Greenodd was the old port, Haverthwaite was the focal point for most of the industries served by the branch, including Backbarrow Ironworks and Lowwood Gunpowder works.

Within a year, Plumpton Junction saw further activity, with the reversal and shunting necessary for the daily goods train onto the Canal branch. This traffic increased further, from 1873 with the construction of the North Lonsdale Ironworks, and in 1876 with the ore and coke trains needed by that works, all delivered over the extended Canal branch. At about this time the Leven sidings were extended eastwards and in 1875 Plumpton crossing was replaced by an overbridge. The crossing house stood into the early 1960s. Not all goods and mineral trains were banked, even at this time. The 1877 working timetable shows that the first two trains of the day from Carnforth were allowed to be split into as many as three sections to get up to Lindal. The bank engines didn't come on duty until 7-00 am.

With the construction of the Bardsea branch, several options were put forward for the new junction. When the line was to continue to Barrow, a passenger station was considered, allowing main line trains (via Bardsea) to connect with passenger trains to Lakeside and to Barrow via Ulverston. In the event, when the Bardsea branch was inspected in June 1883, the new line left the U&L line immediately west of the older junction. A connecting siding linked the southerly of the Leven sidings with the Bardsea branch Down line, over the site of the original signal box. A new box was built by William Gradwell as part of his Bardsea branch contract and had a frame by Easterbrook. It was built on the opposite side of the line, on top of the shallow cutting, above the junctions. The siding into the iron mine was still in place.

No further major changes occurred until the mid 1890s. At the time the First Edition Ordnance Survey map covering the areas around Plumpton Junction was surveyed, before 1890, the siding onto the Plumpton Hall estate and the iron mines were gone. A short runaround loop and a short siding on railway property are shown.

In 1896, the North Lonsdale Iron company obtained a 3-year mineral lease at Plumpton, followed in March 1897 by a lease to quarry limestone. Coincidentally, the FR replaced the signal box at Plumpton Junction with a larger building, on the south side, adjacent to the sidings, opened in February 1897. A 42 ft. turntable was erected in the apex of the Bardsea and main lines, accessed from the Up line on the Bardsea branch. These works followed the implementation of the Regulation of Railways Act on the FR, when many improvements to signalling up and down the line were made necessary. A siding was laid in by the North Lonsdale company, from adjacent to the new Plumpton Junction signal box to a loading platform at the west side of their first quarry. Replacement signal boxes were built at Leven Junction and Greenodd Junction in 1907.

Despite having both mineral and limestone leases on the Plumpton Hall estate, all energy was concentrated on the limestone. For whatever reason, the North Lonsdale company indicated to the Executors of Gradwell that they intended to terminate their contract for Gascow limestone from June 1903. Limestone extraction was in full swing at Plumpton, in the southern end of what became Great Hagg Spring quarry in 1908, by which time the company obtained a 21-year exclusive lease on all limestone on the Plumpton Hall estate, south of the railway. At the time, the limestone was worked in a relatively small way for agricultural use and local building purposes by Ulverston builders Messrs

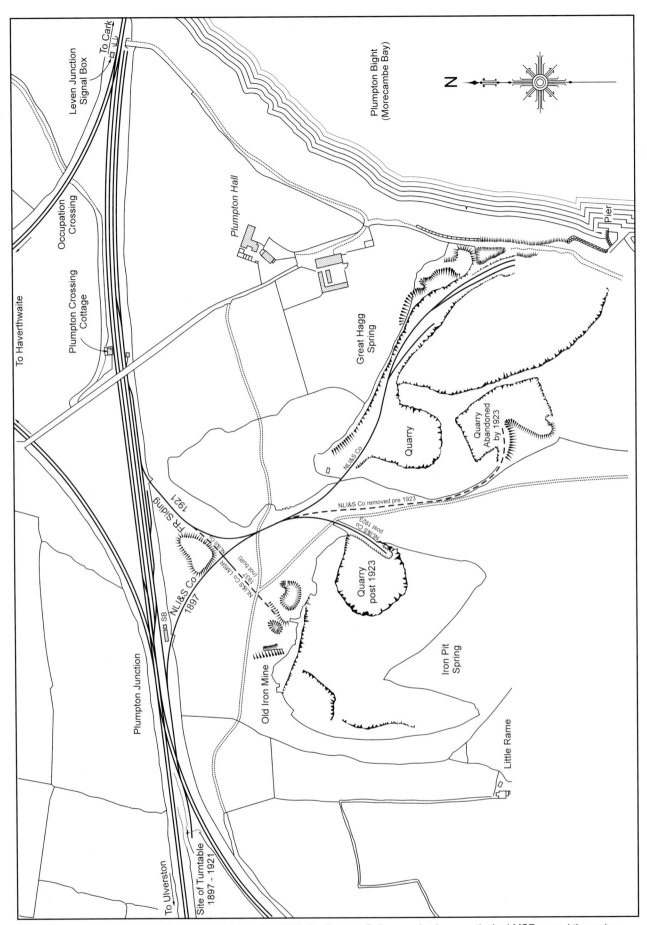

Plumpton Junction circa 1933, *showing how, after 1897, the Furness Railway and subsequently the LMSR served the various sidings into the quarries. There was also a pier on the shore, remote from the railway sidings. Note too the siding added by the FR in 1921 to form a turning triangle, allowing the removal of an earlier turntable used by the bank engines. The triangle remained in use, after the removal of the quarry sidings beyond, until the end of steam.*

(Drawing by Alan Johnstone)

Fleming and Vickers (who vacated the site by March 1910). Over 50,000 tons of limestone was being extracted from Great Hagg Spring quarry in 1908 with over 60,000 tons the following year. The trains of limestone were worked down the Bardsea branch by the FR. As with the ore trains between Park or Lindal and Barrow Ironworks, the North Lonsdale limestone trains were not timetabled. In 1910 the North Lonsdale company proposed to build an aerial ropeway to transport the ore from quarry to works, but this came to naught. Some limestone was also being shipped from a pier (not rail connected) built onto the sands at Plumpton Bight.

In 1920 the turntable at Plumpton Junction was in need of renewal. Instead of replacing it, the cash-strapped railway company built a short siding on the Plumpton Hall estate to form a triangle with the North Lonsdale company's siding. The lease was £1 per year (increased to £3 per year when the LMS renewed the lease in 1926). By 1923 the Great Hagg Spring quarry had been extended northwards and the old loading bay abandoned. The siding was by now diverted into the northern end of the quarry. Quarrying eventually was moved to a new quarry in Iron Pit Spring Wood, to the west of Great Hagg Spring, and the siding moved into a loading bay cut into the quarry floor. In LMS days, the North Lonsdale company was allowed to use their own locomotives to haul the limestone trains.

Maximum output was achieved between July 1928 and June 1929 when over 85,000 tons of limestone were extracted. However, some of the output was destined for other companies. Production dwindled in the months leading to the closure of the North Lonsdale ironworks in October 1931. In the coming years output dropped into the hundreds of tons per annum. Extraction resumed in earnest in early 1937, coinciding with the reopening of two furnaces at North Lonsdale that April. Things were looking up at Plumpton,

and the North Lonsdale company expected to extend the Iron Pit Spring quarry such that a new loading point would be needed on the north side. Agreement was reached in November 1937 for a new siding to the proposed loading bay. This would leave the LMS's side of the triangle of sidings and cross the North Lonsdale's side on the level. The LMS were to lay the points from their siding together with the crossing. The North Lonsdale company would lay the rest of the siding. In the event the points and crossing were laid in by the LMS but no track was put down by the iron company; there was no need. In August 1938 the ironworks stopped pig iron production again and no longer needed the limestone. Quarrying continued until the end of 1939 when it stopped altogether. The limestone rights to Plumpton quarries were eventually acquired by the Barrow ironworks, although there is no indication that any quarrying took place under their tenure.

The 1939-45 war halted any rationalisation at Plumpton or on the Bardsea branch. However, following the post-war financial emergency in Britain, the new British Railways implemented changes. The Leven curve had been last used on 7 August 1939 (August Bank Holiday) after which both Leven Junction and Greenodd Junction signal boxes remained closed. The curve had been used intermittently and usually only in the summer season, since opening in 1869. Leven Junction was eventually closed and points removed in April (Down line) and October (Up line) 1952. At the same time the Bardsea branch was singled and the junction with the U&L main line was simplified. This work was completed in 1953. The track around the Leven curve and the signal boxes at each end were not removed until 1958. The Lakeside branch was singled between Plumpton Junction (actually at a point closer to the site of Greenodd Junction) and Greenodd station in November 1958.

Plumpton Junction. *This view, looking east, dates from circa 1953, following the singling of the Bardsea branch in the right foreground and alteration to the junction layout. The Lakeside branch runs off to the left whilst the North Lonsdale Iron & Steel Company's siding into Plumpton Quarry branches off immediately on the near-side of the signalbox.*

(CRA Photo Library ref. JA1121)

Wraysholme Halt and Crossing, some time in the late 1930s. The fine lower quadrant signal with its concrete post was one of the few reminders of the alterations here during the Great War for the Flookburgh Airship factory. It was installed as part of the signalling to protect the siding, together with the earlier platform and crossing. A signal box stood at the far end of the right hand platform, adjacent to the crossing, for only a few years. (CRA Photo Library/Cdr G Taylor ref. T19A)

The line was one of the last in the country to see revenue-earning main-line steam. This ended with the closure of the London Midland region of British Rail to steam locomotives in early August 1968. By this time coke trains to Barrow and Millom had ceased (to Barrow in 1963 and Millom in that year). The only traffic since 1967 onto the Bardsea branch was fuel oil for the Glaxo works. The Lakeside branch had seen its last passenger train on 5 September 1965, with freight continuing to Haverthwaite until that service was withdrawn from 24 April 1967, following closure of Backbarrow ironworks. The Lakeside branch was removed between Plumpton and Haverthwaite in 1971 after the transfer of stock from Steamtown at Carnforth to the Lakeside & Haverthwaite Railway. The lay-by sidings were shortened and one removed altogether, leaving only a run-around siding for trains down what was effectively a dead-end siding into the Glaxo plant.

The provision of bank engines for goods trains survived the steam era and continued into the mid-1970s.

Glaxo continued to receive its weekly train of oil into the 1980s. This had been an awkward shunt since 1980 when a derailment to the Carnforth – Ulverston – Barrow trip freight train had led to the removal of the crossover road in the main line. From that time the return oil tanks had to be taken to Ulverston for the locomotive to run around its train and head east – five reversals and three loco run-arounds to get some wagons from Carnforth to Glaxo and head back to Carnforth!

In May 1989 BR had agreed to Glaxo using their own locomotive on the branch from Plumpton Junction to their works. A Class 08 shunter was acquired from BR to push the oil tanks down over the canal and into the works. The diesel was banned from the works site. It was not fireproofed and the fireless 0-4-0 had been retired for preservation at the same time. This situation continued until Glaxo stopped receiving oil by rail in April 1994. The branch remained in place for a further six years. In that time only one further

train passed onto the branch: the Royal train was stabled there for a few hours on 22 May 1995. Plumpton Junction signal box was closed on 19 March 2000 and demolished on the following Wednesday. The branch and sidings were removed that May with the redundant point on the main line taken out at the end of September. The closure of the signal box saw one other redundancy – permission was given for Railtrack to remove the wind speed recorder from the east end of Leven Viaduct.

The Great War saw a great demand for airships for the Royal Navy. Vickers at Barrow were early builders of rigid airships and sought to develop their share of the market. After setting up manufacturing sheds at Cavendish Dock and on Walney, Vickers made the decision to move their airship construction facilities from Barrow to a much larger site at Flookburgh. Whether this was to meet demands from the Admiralty for airships, thus attracting government approval, or with a view to a possible post-war development of international airship travel, the development was to be on a massive scale. It should be remembered that the aeroplane was still developing and very few were big enough to carry more than a small payload compared to the more advanced airship. Whatever the long term view, permission was sought from the Admiralty and duly gained on 29 March 1916.

The shed was designed by Sir William Arrol Limited with the contract for construction going to A J Main & Company. The airship shed itself was to be 900 feet long and 300 feet wide, wide enough to hold two lines of airships. To put it in context, the shed, adjacent mooring areas and screens, would, if moved, shelter the whole of the village of Flookburgh with room to spare! Housing for the workers at the new factory was also to be erected. This estate, initially called Flookburgh West, was to be a garden village (originally referred to as the Model Aero Village!) with predominantly semi-detached houses for the skilled workforce required, arranged in a circular pattern.

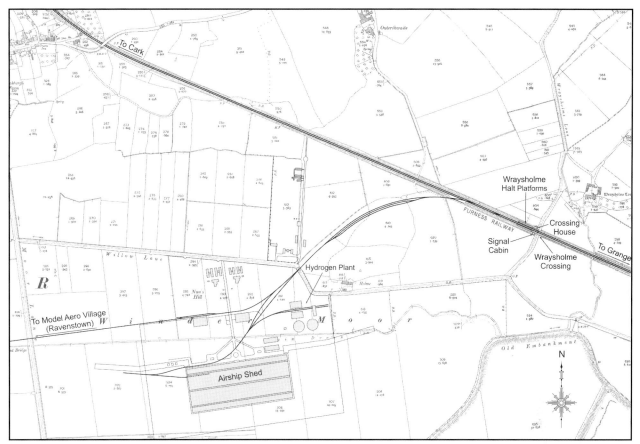

What might have been. *A plan of the sidings into the uncompleted Flookburgh airship factory. Most of the sidings were built for what construction took place at the factory and at the Model Aero Village to the west. Once completed the sidings would serve both the massive airship shed and adjacent hydrogen plant. Today the earthworks adjacent to the main line can be seen heading as far as Willow Lane. RAF Cark was built over the factory site, but the siding to the Model Aero Village (Ravenstown) can be just made out either side of Moor Lane. (Drawing by Alan Johnstone based on an Ordnance Survey map. Crown Copyright Reserved)*

To serve the construction site and with a view to serving the airship factory, a new siding, trailing from the Up line and crossing the Down line, was put in to the west of Wraysholme halt. This was authorized on 29 November 1916 and constructed in the first three months of 1917. The siding, with necessary signalling, was controlled from a new signal box and block post at Wraysholme Crossing, on the south side of the line. The signalling was arranged such that the signals guarding the halt and crossing could be controlled from the ground frame when the signal box was switched out. The new junction and signalling were brought into use on 26 March 1917. Such were the demands of the war effort, the railway works were not approved by the Board of Trade until 7 June 1917. The siding led from the main line to three sidings. Beyond these the line headed west, parallel to the factory, with sidings into the site. It ran across the road running due south of Flookburgh to the site of the new village, allowing construction materials to be delivered directly to the site. A locomotive shed was also provided, presumably to house the contractor's locomotive. The FR timetabled one goods train per day to shunt the siding.

Construction of the airship factory stopped suddenly in September 1917. Progress had been slow, officially due to the unavailability of steel, and little more than the foundations had been laid. Earlier, in June 1917, Vickers had lost the contract for the R37 airship to Short Brothers at Cardington.

Work on the garden village was limited to about a third of the estate as planned: four avenues, each named after a major battle of the war: Somme, Arras, Marne and Jutland. The housing and site passed among various Government departments, who disposed of the houses in 1919 and auctioned off the main factory assets in 1921. The siding from the main line and relevant signalling were closed on 31 August 1922 and removed soon afterwards, leaving Wraysholme halt and crossing looking similar to the position of 1911. The signal box lasted such a short time that it was never photographed and its existence soon forgotten.

Any remaining evidence of the airship factory was removed in 1941 when the Royal Air Force established RAF Cark. This time no special rail facilities were provided. Traffic for the aerodrome arrived from Cark station by road. Airmen and American soldiers housed at the adjacent camp had the option of marching from the station or hiring a bicycle from the enterprising youths of Cark and Flookburgh. Although planned to be a fighter station, following reassessment of defence requirements following the Battle of Britain the base became a Staff Training establishment. The Americans disappeared from the locality prior to D-Day but the RAF station remained in operation until the end of 1945.

Grange. *The ornamental grounds when first planted. In 1865 Alexander Brogden obtained a lease for this land. After completion of the present passenger station and its new approach road, in the background of this photograph, the old approach embankment was removed, and the resultant space was planted and a lake built. The new Grange Hotel, opened in the summer of 1866, overlooks the scene.* *(Courtesy Grange over Sands Photographic Society)*

The Grange Hotel nearing completion. *Workmen are busy preparing the limestone gateposts which still stand at the entrance to the hotel grounds. The advanced state of construction dates this view to early 1866.*

(Courtesy Grange over Sands Photographic Society)

People & Places

5

WITH THE INCREASED accessibility from the more populated areas of Lancashire and the West Riding, no doubt encouraged by the excursions to the area run by the railway companies from the first days of the railway opening, the villages along the line became recognized as places of resort and vacation.

Grange was already appreciated as a seaside resort by a few discerning families and had become the seasonal home of the moderately wealthy. In fact Alexander Brogden bought nearby Holme Island, with its mansion and landscaped grounds, moving in during the summer of 1857. Local entrepreneurs failed to see the potential of the place, or at least were unwilling to invest in hotels or guest houses immediately. Alex Brogden bemoaned the fact that families were found leaving Grange, having only arrived earlier in the day and been unable to find accommodation. It was left to James Ramsden and Alex Brogden to provide the spur of further growth. In October 1863 they set up the Grange Hotel Company Limited, with a capital of £20,000. The company engaged E G Paley to design the handsome hotel overlooking the station. Paley himself held 12 of the £20 shares. The hotel opened in 1866. In the few years previously they had ensured that a handsome station building was erected in 1863 to reflect the potential of the place, replacing the scruffy 9 feet by 24 feet hut which served as a station office. The station approach was improved that year as a new road was built past the entrance and stables of the new hotel, past Blawith and on alongside the railway to the level crossing for Holme Island.

With the new access, the old embankment from the gates of Yewbarrow to the old station crossing was removed. Brogden leased the land not owned by the railway from Benjamin Hall of Yewbarrow in 1865, and during the following year an ornamental lake, with landscaped surrounds, was created on the old Grange Marsh. An 'embankment' was erected by the FR as a public promenade, located between the railway (with views over the sea) and the ornamental grounds.

To further encourage the development of the village, the Grange and Cartmel Gas & Water Company was created, by Act of Parliament, in 1866. Its works were set up at Meathop, adjacent to the river Winster and the railway. The gasworks were quite generous in size for a village, being capable of serving Grange until closure in 1968, when new pipelines were laid in across Cartmel and Furness from a large gasworks near Morecambe. The company provided only a limited supply of water, taken from a weir in the Winster and then run along a narrow channel to the railway embankment, adjacent to the gasworks. Here it was pumped into a pipeline. The pipeline ran south along the railway embankment to Blawith Point, from where it was pumped to a small reservoir or header tank on the adjacent hillside. Not surprisingly, its first customer for gas and probably water was the Grange Hotel, in May 1867. Whilst the gas main extended to serve the rest of the town, few took advantage of the new water supply.

The seed had been sown, and the village then underwent a steady growth. Estimates of population suggest Grange had 130 residents in 1851, with a further 70 ten years later. This grew to 1000 in 1871 and 1700 in 1881. With wealthy residents such as Alexander Brogden, public facilities were not overlooked. The village had gained its church in 1854 and in 1864 the National Schools were opened. The Working Men's Institute opened in 1866.

The village was turning into a small town. A local Board of Health, separate from the older Ulverston Board, was created in 1874. It was this body that started to sort out the problems of supplying water, Grange still being largely reliant on springs and wells. In 1878 they built their first reservoir on the fells at High Newton. The problems of drainage and sewage weren't properly resolved until the turn of the century.

With this growth in houses, boarding houses and private hotels came the parades of shops along Main Street and Kents Bank Road. A Cooperative Society was set up in 1882. The Bank of Liverpool and the Lancaster Bank set up branches. The parish church had been opened before the railway arrived, in 1854, and now further churches were opened for other denominations.

People wanted to visit or live in Grange. However, it was a resort with pretensions. Whist they appreciated the genteel, there was a sigh of relief when the day trippers disappeared. The Morecambe Steamboat Company had built a pier at the end of Bailey Lane, below the church, in 1875, and brought the millworkers of the West Riding on trips from Morecambe. This pier was effectively replaced by another pier adjacent to the Clare House hotel in 1893, a bridge over the railway having been erected there 11 years earlier. Steamer services continued across the bay but ceased around 1911 when silting prevented steamers reaching the pier.

One problem Grange did have was the barrier created by the railway. Access to the sands for bathing and boats was limited to certain points. In the 1870s the Local Board heard a rumour that the Furness Railway was to close several level crossings around the station, to allow for its expansion. These crossings, at the north end of the station platforms and at Blawith Point, were the best places to access the beach and bathing machines. The Board of Trade were consulted but had no powers to act. The railway company and Local Board discussed the issue and compromise was reached. With some funding by local men, the grand footbridge at Blawith Point and the subway at the station were constructed in 1877. At the same time the low road to Lindale was moved about 20 yards to the north between the Grange Hotel entrance to beyond Blawith.

With the building of the main sewer in 1902-4 along the railway embankment, and perhaps inspired by Bazelgette's Embankment along the Thames in London (built over a major sewer), local philanthropists and the new Urban District Council built a promenade, running from Blawith Point almost to Cart Lane, then still a separate hamlet from the main town.

This growth between the appearance of the railway and the Great War was mirrored by similar developments from Silverdale in the east to Kents Bank in the west. Here the developments were due more to local influence.

Arnside saw the most significant growth after Grange as a resort. Like Grange, it had, in the eighteenth century, been where a 'Tide Waiter' or local customs officer had lived and worked, collecting duty from ships headed for Milnthorpe, which often could only make the journey so far up the Kent estuary that goods had to be taken on by lighter.

By the time the railway was built, that traffic was dwindling. Arnside was a scattered settlement, of which the Fighting Cocks Inn and a few other houses and cottages faced the sea. The village was already a place of resort, and, as at Grange, several large houses were occupied by solicitors, merchants and ship owners from Liverpool and elsewhere. The only real industry there was Crossfield's boat building and joinery. The Crossfield family had set up business in about 1830 and were boat builders from 1838 until 1951, their output concentrating on rowing and small sailing craft such as Morecambe Bay shrimpers, a few of

Arnside. An 1890s view from the railway embankment. The Crown Hotel on the left had previously been called the Fighting Cocks. In recent years the original name has been restored. The pier erected by the railway in settlement of the dispute with Kendal Chamber of Commerce stands to the right.
(Courtesy Grange over Sands Photographic Society)

which still survive around the country. Branches of the family also set up the first post office and grocery store. Most villagers lived in houses and farms scattered over the land towards the county boundary. Its population was similar to that of the area which became Grange Urban District but growth was slower, only reaching 850 by 1900. It gained its parish church in 1866, but the village school didn't appear until 1874, under the 'British' system (organized under the British & Foreign Bible Society). This was replaced by one on the 'National' system (Church of England) in 1886.

As well as the villas, boarding houses and private hotels, Arnside became home to several private schools, the first appearing in 1884. Some were longer lived than others, with the final one not closing until the 1970s.

The first purpose-built shop in the village was a Crossfield establishment of 1863. Retail development didn't really start until about 1880; the Bank of Liverpool also set up the first bank in the same year.

Whilst Arnside gained its stone jetty in 1861, it was little used commercially. When the Morecambe Steamboat Company began its cross-bay services, it built its own pier, as it had at Grange. This lasted until damaged by storms around 1908.

The low road across the seaward side of Arnside was literally along the shore. It wasn't until 1897 that it was raised and the promenade built. In fact, before the building of the Ulverstone & Lancaster Railway, the road to the village was from Beetham, with its parish church. A road from Storth along the shore was built as part of the compensation for not opening the sliding bridge on the Kent Viaduct to allow ships to Sandside. The present Storth road was built, again by the railway, when the branch line from Arnside to Sandside and Hincaster Junction was built in the early 1870s. Between Arnside and Storth this followed the course of the older railway-built road. The new road branched off the old road towards Beetham, passing under the railway by a narrow bridge. This was widened and the road lowered in 1912.

Like Grange, Arnside relied for many years on its springs and wells for water supply. For a number of years an unsatisfactory supply came from Grange, following the building of the High Newton reservoir. It would be 1906 before a proper water supply was built, with a reservoir at Lupton. A H Strongitharm, the Barrow Civil Engineer, was Inspector of Works for the project. Two years earlier an attempt was made to set up a gasworks, to the north of the station goods yard on Storth Road. The works were abandoned by 1907 and only the Manager's house remains to mark the site. Electricity was produced in Arnside in 1910 by Thomas Wilkinson, who went on to set up an electricity generator in Grange in 1912.

Of the various wealthy residents of Arnside, the name known to many railway enthusiasts is Thomas W Worsdell. Whilst works manager of the LNWR's Crewe works, Worsdell had 'Stoneycroft' built in 1879. Following his retirement as Locomotive Superintendent of the North Eastern Railway in 1890, Worsdell came to live at Arnside until his death in 1916.

Silverdale also benefited from its location close to the sea, but avoided sea-front development. Instead the villas and houses were scattered across the village. Silverdale, like Grange, had been the property of Cartmel Priory in mediaeval times. Cartmel had gained the vill together with fishing rights in Haweswater in the reign of Richard I and established a cell of monks there in 1233. At the time the railway was built it was recognised as a resort, with the popular authoress, Mrs Gaskell, holidaying there. It already had a church (a chapel of Warton parish church) built in 1829, but this would be replaced by the present structure in 1886. It remains pretty much as Niklaus Pevsner described it in the 1960s, 'the most pleasant, i.e. the least crowded, the least urban seaside resort in this area'. This remains true today. Whilst it has its modest hotels, there is no promenade or municipal gardens.

The smallest 'resort' was Kents Bank. This hamlet, at the point where the cross-sands road from Lancaster reached terra firma for a few miles, already had an inn. John Brogden stayed at Abbot Hall, the seaside villa of J S Young, on occasion whilst his Ulverstone & Lancaster Railway was being built (ultimately cutting Abbot Hall off from the sea). Villa development commenced in the 1870s when Kentsford Road was built from the station northwards towards the old road from Allithwaite to Cart Lane (home of the Guide over the Kent Sands). There was even Brogden involvement with this: Alexander Brogden's son James built Kentsford House here before the great Brogden family bankruptcies a few years later. It would be well into the 20th century before the real growth of Kents Bank took place, with the post-war growth in housing.

One resident of note at Kents Bank, for a period during the Great War, was a young engineer working for Vickers at Barrow by the name of Barnes Wallis.

Outside Ulverston, the largest population centre originally served by the railway was the township of Lower Holker, that is the villages of Cark, Flookburgh and Holker. Flookburgh, as we have seen, was an important place in times past, developed on the cross-bay road by the monks of Cartmel. With the opening of the railway this passing trade disappeared overnight and Flookburgh settled down as an agricultural and fishing village, seeing little real growth until the 20th century and the arrival of the proposed airship

Silverdale. *This 1890s panorama of the village highlights the rural nature of the area served by the railway. The new parish church of 1886 stands to the left with the main village off to its right in the distance. Morecambe Bay is off in the right distance. (Courtesy Grange over Sands Photographic Society)*

factory towards the end of the Great War. A model village was planned for its workers and, before the scheme was abandoned, about a third of the planned estate was built. This became Ravenstown, named after a nearby farm. In the 1940s, the airship factory site, together with much of the East Plain estate, to the south of Flookburgh, was turned over to the military, with the RAF setting up their Cark air station and the Army housing the inevitable American troops there.

Cark's industrial hey-day had passed by the time the railway was built. The village was still dominated by its mill, although this had been, since 1815, a corn mill. Its owners imported grain from around Britain via the village wharf until that was cut through by the railway in 1853. The mill remained in operation until destroyed by a massive fire in 1935.

The railway served as an enabler to the needs of the community but had little need to develop it. The arrival of the railway saw the building of the Station Hotel at the station gates and allowed agricultural auctions to take place near to the station. Whilst the first was held in 1858 in a field alongside the station, a small auction mart was later developed in the village. Its appearance led to as many as three banks setting up branches in the village, although these tended to open on market day only! The community was big enough for its own Cooperative Society, set up in

1872, with a shop in the centre of Cark and with a later branch in Flookburgh. This survived as an independent organization until it was wound up in 1964. The spiritual needs of the area were served by Flookburgh chapel. The Wesleyan Methodists didn't erect a chapel at Cark until 1914. They had previously met in one of the houses adjacent to the large corn mill set aside for the meetings.

Whilst gas never reached the villages of Lower Holker until the arrival of North Sea gas, electricity arrived in the Great War. The Cark and District Electric Supply Co. Ltd. was set up in 1915. Its works were in Flookburgh, in farm buildings once owned by James Stockdale and rented by John Brogden during the construction of the railway! The works were taken over about 1930 by Barrow Corporation.

The third village, Holker, had by the 1850s become purely an estate village for Holker Hall, home to William Cavendish, Earl of Burlington and from January 1858, 7th Duke of Devonshire. As we have seen, this Cavendish, with his sons and grandsons, were significant investors in the railway and in the development of nearby Barrow, among other places. They also made extensive use of the railway, especially when Holker was only one of several houses used by the Devonshires. Then full trains were used to take the Duke, family, entourage, servants, luggage, horses, carriages et al between Rowsley (for Chatsworth), Cark (for Holker Hall), Bolton Abbey and occasionally Eastbourne. Extensive use

Flookburgh. *Looking west along the old over-sands road at the centre of the village. On the left stands the market cross, erected in the 19th century by the village vicar. His chapel stands in the trees behind the house on the left (its site is now the village square). On the right stands the Hope & Anchor Inn, one of many inns and hotels once in the village. (Author's Collection)*

Holker Hall. *Home of William Cavendish, 2nd Earl of Burlington and later 7th Duke of Devonshire. The Ulverstone & Lancaster skirts the southern edge of the Holker Estate. Fire ravaged through the west wing of the Hall on 1871. To save himself from the conflagration, Devonshire had to jump from his bedroom window. Paley & Austin of Lancaster designed the replacement, which dominates the right hand of the photograph. To the left stands the long-demolished conservatory, built using panels designed by Joseph Paxton and better known in their use at Chatsworth and for the Crystal Palace. (Author's Collection)*

was also made on an individual basis. As well as regular journeys to Ulverston, for the Board of Guardians meetings, and Barrow to visit Cavendish businesses, the railway allowed longer journeys. In the 1870s Lord Frederick Cavendish, when standing as MP for that area, could attend hustings in Keighley, travelling there and back from Cark by train in the day! The station also saw the great and the good on their way to Holker, including royalty and the statesmen of the day.

The arrival of the Ulverstone & Lancaster Railway was the spur to the transformation of Carnforth and its neighbour, Warton. Both are ancient settlements but it was at Warton that the parish church was established. Whilst Warton developed as an agricultural village, with its links to the Washington family, Carnforth was influenced by its place on transport routes. It has always been on the high road between Lancashire and Westmorland. The coming of the Garstang and Heron Syke Turnpike in 1751 saw coaching inns appear in the village. The arrival of the Lancaster Canal in 1797 improved transport links further: a wharf was provided adjacent to the turnpike south of the village. 1818-20 saw the construction of the Ulverston & Carnforth Turnpike, which actually ran from Greenodd to Levens Bridge and from Milnthorpe to Low Hyning, north of Carnforth. The Ulverston Trust's act allowed the Heron Syke Trust's road to be diverted between Tewitfield and Carnforth, thus providing the route of the modern A6 to the west of the old village. Further inns appeared.

The arrival of the Lancaster & Carlisle Railway in 1846 had little initial impact. It was merely a new form of transport to add to the coaching routes and canal passing through the village. It only needed and got a 'second class' station. The need to pass trains from one railway company to another led to the gradual development of exchange sidings and locomotive sheds, all requiring an increasing number of staff. These in turn needed housing for themselves and their families. The availability of limestone on Warton Crag, of cheap haematite from Furness and coal from south Lancashire by the new railways, made Carnforth the ideal site for a group of Manchester investors to set up an ironworks, the Carnforth Haematite Iron Company Ltd. Production at the ironworks began in 1866. This needed more sidings on the railway, more railway workers and of course workers for the ironworks itself. Thus Carnforth was transformed from a village of about 294 in 1851 into a thriving small town of over 1000 by 1871. Warton was not left behind and had a population of 1035 in the same year. Ten years further on and the populations were 1879 and 1471 respectively.

The railway station and ironworks both drew Carnforth and Warton towards each other, especially with the building of the industrial settlement of Millhead (better known to older residents as Dudley, from the early ironworkers who came to the area from the Black Country). At the same time, however, they formed a very substantial barrier to their actually merging. Carnforth's parade of shops, named Market Street, was built along the existing road to Warton west from the turnpike to the station. Its Cooperative Society (established in 1885) grew to the extent it was capable of extending its branches to Arnside and Grange (whose own society was taken over in 1904). The Society remained independent until absorbed in 1970. Gas and waterworks were provided in the 1870s. The spiritual and educational needs of the populace didn't go unnoticed. The village gained its own parish church in 1873 whilst the Wesleyan Methodists had set up their chapel in 1870, the Primitive Methodists opened theirs in 1873 and the Congregationalist Chapel appeared in 1882. There had been a school in Carnforth since 1849 but this was extended in 1872.

The housing for iron workers and for FR and Midland Railway men was built in both Carnforth and Warton, close to both ironworks and the railway yards. The LNWR built its own housing stock in 1896-8, to the south of the town, between the former turnpike and the railway and close to its engine sheds.

Carnforth was to lose its ironworks in 1929, the site later being used as an ordnance factory and in the later 20th century as an industrial estate. The railway meantime continued to be a heavy employer until the 1960s when Carnforth's railway presence was cut back with the final closure of the locomotive shed in 1968, and the demolition of the main-line platforms two years later prior to electrification of the West Coast Main Line. Meanwhile through the 20th century road transport increased, with the turnpike road becoming the busy A6 road to Carlisle. Carnforth became one of many bottlenecks on that busy transport artery, leading to Lancashire County Council building one of Britain's first motorways, the M6 Lancaster (and Carnforth) bypass, opened in 1958. The motorway has, of course been extended south and later north to become the M6 we know today. The bottleneck wasn't totally removed since for many years afterwards, increasing numbers of visitors travelled by road, rather than railway, to Morecambe and those coming from the north still had to use the A6 through the town.

Stations & Sidings

6

Grange Station and approach, circa 1863. The rebuilding of the original station has started, with the goods shed in an advanced state of construction. The original wooden station office is still in use. The station and its crossing, giving access to the sands, are approached by an embankment. The cottage and barn beyond were at one time a Dame School. A box-like contraption in the foreground, alongside its wheels, is either a bathing machine or contractor's bothy. Within a couple of years this scene would have changed completely.
(Courtesy Grange over Sands Photographic Society)

AS DESCRIBED EARLIER, the primary objective of the railway was to get iron ore eastwards from Furness and coke westwards to the growing ironworks at Barrow. The goods facilities to the villages along the line appear basic but were probably adequate for small rural settlements with little industry, where bringing in goods and supplies was as important as any products being shipped out. However, as time went on the railways became more widely used, and the villages grew as a result of the improved communications on offer.

The original stations provided were typical of the period and, by later standards, fairly rudimentary. These were at Cark, Kents Bank, Grange and Silverdale, as well as the junctions at Ulverston and Carnforth. All trains could be passed at Cark and Grange. Cark and Silverdale stations were the first to be completed. Both were provided with sturdy, workmanlike station houses on the Down (Ulverston) side, providing accommodation for the station master and his family as well as the station office. Both had sidings for a coal yard and a cattle or loading ramp. Cark had additional sidings, on the Up (Carnforth) side and a good-sized warehouse. No shelter was provided on its Up platform. Access to Cark station was from the Down side only, halfway between Cark and Flookburgh villages. Silverdale station was built directly adjacent to a lane linking the roads from the village to Warton and Beetham.

In 1860 the U&LR Directors saw fit to maintain their rolling stock themselves rather than paying the Furness Railway or the Railway Carriage Company to do it. In the second half of that year they built a wagon works at Cark. Here the 600 or more ore wagons leased by the company could be maintained. In later years wagons were actually built here. This probably accounts for some of the sidings the Directors reported on during 1860 and 1861.

Whilst well known for its fish traffic, one forgotten commodity shipped at Cark was gunpowder. Soon after the railway opened siding facilities were provided for the Low Wood Gunpowder Company, allowing them to distribute their products by rail as well as by sea. The gunpowder company used its own wagons for this traffic. Cark lost its gunpowder traffic after a not uneventful decade, following the opening of Haverthwaite station in September 1869. On more than one occasion accidents, fortunately of a minor nature, occurred.

When the railway arrived at Grange it would appear that the U&LR directors didn't quite know what to do, given its potential as a resort but with the absence of hotels or similar accommodation. As well as being a passing place for trains, a goods and engineers siding was put in and a wooden locomotive shed erected, presumably for the Brogdens' private locomotive which had been used during the later stages of construction. However, facilities for the station staff were in a small wooden hut, accessed by a lane across an embankment over the erstwhile Grange Marsh.

Kents Bank was the most basic station of all, having just a platform on the Up side. As the Inspecting Officer had noted, no station offices had been provided! A wooden hut was eventually constructed to shelter the station master, who also had to deal with the gates of the adjacent level crossing. The opening of the railway coincided with the death of the landlord of the nearby hotel. With no passing coaching trade (that had been killed precisely on the opening of the railway) and no publican, the hotel remained closed and little if any traffic was handled. The nearest village was Allithwaite, about a mile away, but the only access to the station was down a steep hill. Otherwise there were a few houses and the mansion, Abbot Hall. The U&LR closed the station after publication

Ulverston Station in the 1860s. *The FR terminus of 1855 stands above the later through station built for the opening of the U&LR. This was, in turn, replaced by the present station in 1874. The Furness company owned the whole station, with the U&LR being tenants. The left-hand office building alongside the terminus was erected to accommodate the U&LR staff. The station signal and signalman's shelter stand at the top of the ramp to the Up platform.*
(From The North Lonsdale Magazine)

of the timetable for April 1858. The U&LR board decided that it could reopen from November 1858 on condition that the hotel was let and there was some chance of business. In fact Kents Bank didn't appear again in the public timetable until May 1859. Whether the hotel was let is debatable since, in March 1860, J S Young of Abbot Hall was advertising the tenancy for immediate occupation. A passing loop appears to have been put in at Kents Bank before the doubling of the line in 1863.

Ulverston was always owned by the Furness Railway, since, as mentioned earlier, the U&LR started at the Prince's Street bridge. The Furness had opened their line to Ulverston to goods on 4 April 1854 and to passengers on 7 June. At first a temporary wooden passenger station had been built whilst the permanent station was under construction. The wooden building didn't last long, being blown down in a gale on New Years Day 1855. Its successor was a much more imposing train shed with a single platform and offices in matching single-storey buildings at the wings. Standing on the hillside above Ulverston, with few houses to hide it, the Furness let the town know the railway had arrived! It was here that an extension was made to the ticket office in order to be able to deal with the growth in passengers using the station following the opening of the U&LR. As well as the passenger shed, the Furness had provided a sizeable goods yard with coal drops and a warehouse.

With the opening of the U&LR, arrangements were made for the U&LR to pay £350 per annum rent for Ulverston station with the two companies sharing the operating costs. Trains appear to have used the Furness Railway's terminus at first until the U&LR line platforms were ready. The platforms provided were in the cutting below the terminus and west of Prince's Street bridge, connected by a footbridge. At the western end of the Down platform was a loading dock for gentlemen's carriages together with a wooden two-road carriage shed. In 1860 covered platforms were authorised by the Furness for the low-level station. The canopies over both platforms had simple iron supports and brackets with none of the flourishes that would be seen later on the Furness. At some time in the 1860s the low level platforms were almost doubled in length towards the west.

Meanwhile, at Carnforth, more definite arrangements had been made with the Lancaster & Carlisle company. Here a single platform had been provided for the U&LR to the west of Tite's station lodge. Now there were to be additional offices, and the passenger facilities capped off by a train shed over the U&LR platform and track. Interchange sidings were provided for the goods and mineral traffic, controlled by a signal box. In 1861 a loco shed and turntable were provided between the railway and the Warton road for the Furness.

Silverdale. *Looking towards Carnforth on 27 August 1957. The siding to the left runs behind the Up platform into a small enclosed coal yard, known as Gillow's siding. The loading dock, station house and the remains of the low Down platform date from U&LR days.*
(CRA Photo Library ref. PEJ902)

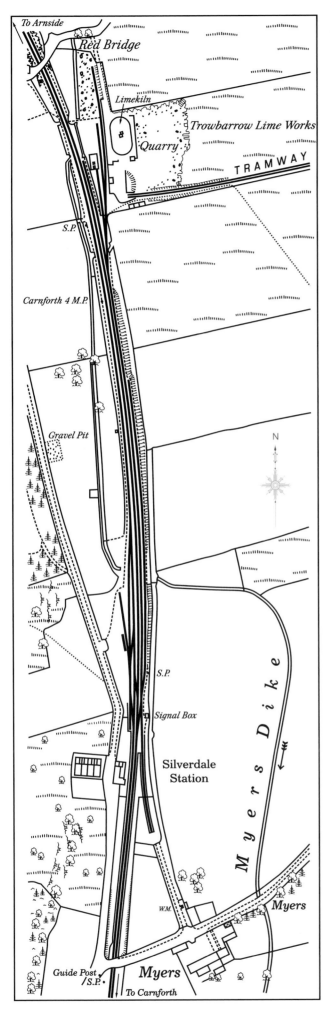

Silverdale Station and Trowbarrow Lime Works based on the 1891 Ordnance Survey. Note how the road north from Myers Farm had been diverted to avoid the station site. Trowbarrow quarry was to the east of the Lime Works, connected by an incline plane, annotated as a tramway on the map.

(Drawing by Alan Johnstone, Crown Copyright Reserved)

As has been already mentioned, there was no intention to provide a station at Arnside at first. At the time the village had ceased, suddenly some would say, to be a port and its inn and houses remained facing the sea. By the May of 1858 the directors authorised the provision of a siding at the Carnforth end of what is now the Down platform. This was to placate the Admiralty and the Kendal Chamber of Trade and avoid providing the opening section of the Kent Viaduct. By July a petition had been drawn up and presented to the U&LR board requesting the provision of passenger station. Arnside was added as a conditional stop for some trains from the July timetable but a platform wasn't authorised until November. Arnside didn't get a place in the main timetable until May 1859, along with Kents Bank. A station house was soon provided. Because of the location of the platform, this had to be built on the side of the embankment there. Thus, although not identical to those provided at either Cark or Silverdale or the level crossing lodges, it included design similarities.

With the arguments over the provision of the opening drawbridge on the Kent viaduct settled, the U&LR found itself obliged to provide a 60 ft. long pier downstream of the viaduct in lieu of Sandside and to build a road from Arnside station to the Dixies Inn. Kendal Chamber of Commerce had proposed these in February 1859 and agreement was reached 17 months later and confirmed at an Admiralty Enquiry into the Navigation of the Leven and Kent estuaries on 7 August 1861. The road crossed the railway by the level crossing located at the Grange end of the station platform, at a point where the current access to the station exists today.

Plans of Grange station in the early days show the pencil outline of a building of layout similar to those at Cark and Silverdale. The Brogdens and their secretary James Ramsden had grander plans. They envisaged a new passenger station just north of the original platforms. E G Paley, the Lancaster Architect, was commissioned to design a station building suitable for a genteel resort. One of his suggestions had a façade more suited to a pleasure palace at Blackpool. The successful design, incorporating two houses, with ticket office, waiting rooms and other facilities was, and is, much more in keeping with the place, being similar in style to the Grange Hotel, also by Paley, being built across the road. A goods shed, in what was to become the standard FR design, had been provided in early 1863 before work started on the permanent station building. These had been announced in the Ulverston Advertiser during November 1862. A new approach road was built and the station level crossing moved to the northern end of the platforms. This allowed the old crossing and approach to be removed and Grange Marsh be redeveloped as the Ornamental Grounds. The approach road actually ran on alongside the railway as far as Holme Island crossing, allowing the Alex Brogden family easier access into the village and the station.

As already mentioned, the Ulverstone & Lancaster company had doubled two sections of its line, firstly from the Leven viaduct up to Ulverston, completed in August 1860, followed by the section from the east end of the viaduct to Cark, completed in July 1861. In 1863 the Furness Railway decided to complete the double line. J Roscoe Allen of Preston won the tender for doubling the line from Cark to Carnforth in February 1863. He had to complete the Arnside to Grange section by that June and the remainder a month later! The final sections to be completed were the Leven and Kent viaducts. This work was carried out by W & J Galloway, whose tender for £16,500 was for completion of both viaducts by August 1863. Additional platforms were provided at Arnside and Silverdale. As elsewhere, no shelters were provided on the second platform at these places.

The period around the time of the FR takeover of the U&LR also saw the provision of proper lodges for the public level crossings. These were of a new design, noticably different to those built in the 1850s on the Furness and Coniston railways. During 1864-65, lodges were built at the crossings at Silverdale, Black Dyke, Kents Bank, Wraysholme, Flookburgh, Cark (or Crookwheel) and Plumpton. That at Kents Bank also served as the station office.

With its location at the eastern side of the Kent, Arnside became a strategic point for several railway schemes. In 1862 the first scheme was submitted to Parliament, the Kendal and Ulverstone Junction Railway. This was to run along the eastern shore of the Kent estuary, then inland to a possible junction with the L&CR at Hincaster, before running north alongside the Lancaster Canal to terminate near the canal basin in Kendal. The Furness and LNW railways objected to the scheme and it was withdrawn at the House of Commons Committee stage, before getting Assent.

It wasn't long before another scheme appeared, this time towards Milnthorpe and Barbon, on the L&CR main line and Ingleton branch respectively. Originally part of the East & West Yorkshire Union Railway (which would stretch as far east as Northallerton), this western section became the Furness & Yorkshire Union Railway, with plans submitted to Parliament in November 1864. The Furness and the LNWR naturally objected to this potential loss of revenue for Coke traffic from the North East. The promotors were persuaded to drop the eastern portion of their scheme and hand over the section from Arnside to Milnthorpe to the Furness. The FR renamed this as the Furness & Lancaster & Carlisle Union Railway before the line was authorised. The FR were given running powers over the L&CR from Milnthorpe to Tebay. Just over a year later the Furness submitted a Bill to, among other things, formally absorb and abandon the F&L&CUR scheme in favour of a route similar to the Kendal & Ulverstone Junction scheme from Arnside to Hincaster. It was to be another nine years before the line would open.

In 1867 the Furness & Midland Joint Railway opened from Wennington to Carnforth. Since this line was designed to facilitate traffic between Furness and the West Riding, no direct access into Carnforth passenger station was provided. A short-lived passenger station was provided on this line adjacent to Warton Road when the line opened, but this was replaced from 1868 by a station to the west of the junction between the joint line and the Furness. This was known as Carnforth F&M and had a timber station building of a design by E G Paley, similar to several he had designed for the North Western Railway and a taste of his company's future designs for the Furness. Access was by a new road linking Carnforth and the Warton to Silverdale turnpike alongside and over the river Keer. Exchange sidings extended between the old and new F&M stations, in which the Midland built a loco shed.

Change came to the Ulverston & Lancaster section as the Furness Railway reached its financial zenith. The construction of the FR's Hincaster branch, started in the summer of 1874, coincided with the upgrading of facilities

The village goods yard: Arnside in the 1950s. This yard was located in the angle between the U&LR main line and the Hincaster branch, and ended against the Arnside – Storth road (itself built by the railway to replace the earlier railway-built road removed on building the branch). As can be seen, the yard consisted of three sidings, a goods shed and weigh bridge. Behind the trees on the left is the site of the short-lived Arnside Gas Works. (CRA Photo Library ref. JA0389)

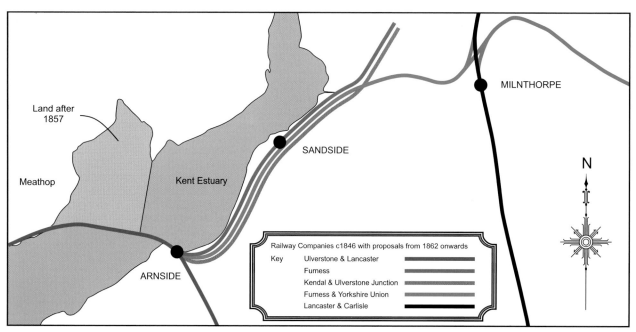

Branch lines, both projected and built, which would have connected to the U&L line at Arnside. Note the common route north from Arnside. (Drawn by Alan Johnstone)

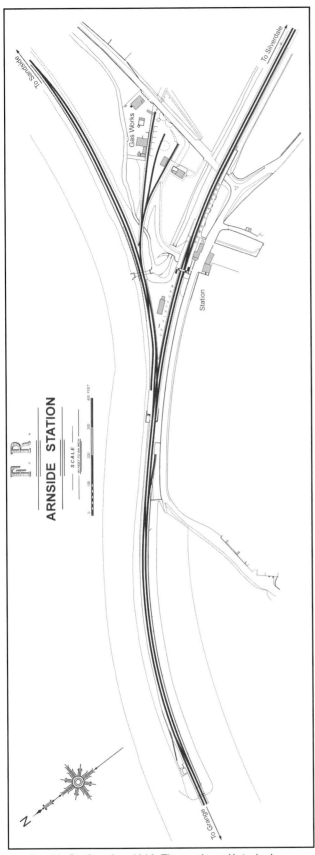

F.R.

ARNSIDE STATION

Arnside Station circa 1914. The goods yard is tucked away between the main line and the Hincaster branch with the short-lived gasworks alongside. Note the lay-by siding running from the branch almost to the signalbox, but never connected to the lines at that end. Note also the bridge over the dyke and adjacent to the footbridge. This was built by the U&LR as part of their road from Arnside to Storth, replaced in the 1870s by the one further south.
(Drawing by Alan Johnstone based on a Cumbria CRO document, ref. WT-BR-1-17)

along the U&LR section. As well as the addition of the branch and its additional platform, opened on 26 June 1876, the opportunity was taken to replace Arnside's rather inadequate goods facilities – the siding of 1858 together with another at the western end of the Down platform – with a proper goods yard. The location of the station on an embankment precluded much development at that level, although a carriage landing was constructed in 1880 adjacent to the junction and closer to the village than the other facilities. The new goods yard was accessed by rail from the branch and terminated at the new road from Arnside to Storth. This had become necessary because of the construction of the Hincaster branch over the old road. The new road also allowed the closure of the station level crossing. The goods yard included a simple goods warehouse, smaller than those at Cark and Grange, more a stone version of those built in wood at Eskmeals and Sellafield. Later a weighbridge was added at the entrance from the Storth road. Up on the junction platform a building housing waiting and toilet facilities was erected. It was of timber frame construction and had some similarities to E G Paley's early railway work. It was, however, totally dissimilar to Paley and Austin's more modern designs being built elsewhere on the Furness.

The 1870s were a period of boom for the Furness Railway and a great deal of capital was expended, not just on Barrow's docks, but on modernising and extending stations all along the system.

Ulverston received significant investment. Architects Paley and Austin were commissioned in 1872 to design the *magnum opus* of their Furness Railway designs. Whilst other stations were to get buildings in wood or brick or rubble stone, Ulverston was to have sandstone ashlar. The architects produced something combining Italianate with a simple eccledsiatical style, having features seen and used in previous FR work. Unlike its predecessor, the buildings were to be in the cutting accessed by a wide approach road, rather than up at road level, and therefore height was in important factor in the design.

The large main block housed a lofty booking hall and waiting room at platform level with apartments for the station master above. At its east side was a lofty tower, suggesting a church with campanile. Unfortunately no clock was provided for almost 30 years. The FR were impressed with the design and, in March 1873, the tender of Robert Clarkson of Carnforth was accepted to build the structure.

To the west of the main block, an arcade of station offices and waiting rooms were provided. These fronted the platform with arches filled with wood and glass screens, similar to those at Grange and Barrow Town stations. Ground level windows were distinctive, with monograms and dates on the approach side. A glass canopy sheltered passengers entering the station. The ornamental ironwork included a floral monogram.

Within the station tall, light and airy glass canopies covered the platforms. Fine octagonal columns rose up with brackets, including the FR monogram, to carry the opaque glass. Due to the rising gradient through the station and in order to provide a level roof line, the columns at the western end were much taller than at the east, this accident to the perspective making the roof and platforms appear much longer.

The platform layout followed a pattern almost unique to the Furness. Besides the usual Down platform, there was an island platform between Up and Down lines, connected to the main platform via a subway. Thus passengers could cross from a through train to a Lakeside branch train or vice versa with ease. It was also to provide dangerous temptation to generations of schoolboy long-jumpers when the station staff weren't looking.

Construction of the main parts of the new station lasted through 1874 and into 1875 with the fish house at the west end being added in 1876. The approach road wasn't completed until 1879. At some point a

Looking along the Hincaster branch towards Arnside station, circa 1885. The arrangement of the home signals to the right of the photograph suggests the nearby Kent viaduct was being re-decked and only a single line passed over the viaduct for the duration of the works. At this time, although the Arnside-Storth road had been diverted, the main line platforms were still staggered either side of the former level crossing, seen to the right of the stone-built station building. The small bridge to its right carried the siding leading into the station goods yard. The half-timbered building on the junction platform was erected for the opening of the Hincaster branch, and differs in style to other half-timbered buildings designed by Paley and Austin of Lancaster for the FR. It was replaced in 1914 by a brick structure which survives. (Photograph by Gilbert Wilson of Grange, Author's Collection)

refreshment room was added on the main platform, against a screen wall. Other outbuildings stood at each end of the platform.

Up at the good yard, during 1876-8, the arrangement of sidings was stretched to the west, with additional ones provided. A large stable block and cart sheds, again by Paley and Austin, together with a cottage were built at the yard gates. The northern wing of the old station was given a second storey, thus providing a further cottage.

Expansion and upgrading of facilities at the other stations followed in 1876-79. The least affected was Kents Bank, which only gained a goods siding, whilst at Silverdale additonal sidings were provided together with a timber waiting shelter and toilet block, by Paley and Austin, on the Up platform.

At Cark substantial changes were made, mainly on the Up side. The goods loop behind the Up platform was removed to allow that platform to be extended. A new block of station offices was provided, including Ladies' and Gentlemen's waiting rooms, lavatories, booking office and porters room together with a large open waiting area and booking hall, fronted by a timber and glass canopy. A new approach road was built from Cark village giving access to the new booking office and new goods facilities. These were built to the north of the station. The new yard included a cattle dock with loading ramp and a substantial coal yard. On the Down side a new tank house with lavatories was provided, to supply the water crane for Down trains. The older tank house on the Up side had suffered from subsidence, and, with its reduced capacity, could no longer

Cark. A 1930s view of Cark station looking towards Carnforth. Whilst the Station House, down platform and goods shed date from U&LR days, the handsome Up-platform building with its canopy, together with the signal box beyond the good shed, dated from the 1870s. In the trees to the right stands one of the two tank houses at Cark. As well as providing a head of water for the water crane at the end of the down platform, the building included a Gentlemen's lavatory and acted as a store for shrimps. This noisome commodity was one of the key traffics from Cark for many years. (CRA Photo Library ref. PA0042)

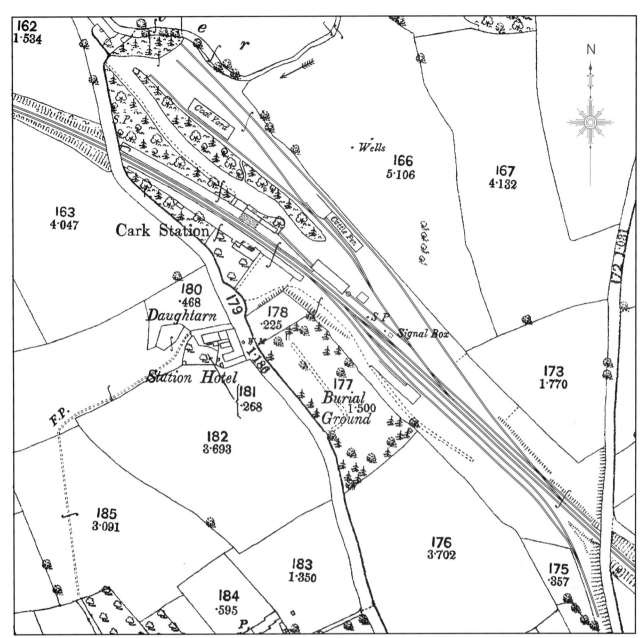

Cark. The station circa 1891. Cark village is to the north of the station with Flookburgh to the south. Field 176 was prone to flooding, which occasionally extended over the whole station area at track level.

(From an Ordnance Survey map of 1891, Crown Copyright Reserved)

Cark. This 1930s view looking towards Ulverston shows the eastern end of Cark station. On the left is the pair of down lay-by sidings, with the small cattle dock beyond. On the up side, the right-hand siding was the up refuge siding, extending the full length of the goods yard. Note the tank house behind the signalbox. Due to the railway being on an embankment across marshy ground in most of the area in view, the building subsided and for most of its useful life was never able to hold its potential capacity of water for the Up-side water crane. (CRA Photo Library ref. PA0043)

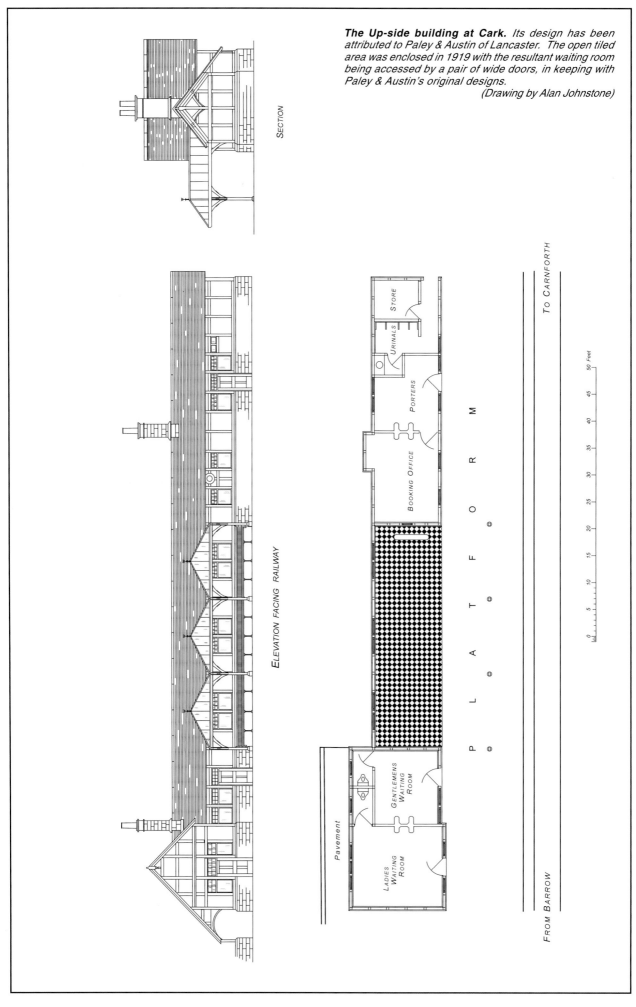

The Up-side building at Cark. *Its design has been attributed to Paley & Austin of Lancaster. The open tiled area was enclosed in 1919 with the resultant waiting room being accessed by a pair of wide doors, in keeping with Paley & Austin's original designs.*

(Drawing by Alan Johnstone)

Grange station in the 1880s. The stationmaster and his staff, together with the bookstall manager, a few invited 'passengers' and platelayers pose for Gilbert Wilson, the photographer. The 'passengers' are probably friends of the photographer as they appear in other photographs taken on the same day. (Courtesy Grange over Sands Photographic Society, Dodgson collection)

supply the water cranes on both Down and Up sides. The opportunity was taken to eliminate Flookburgh level crossing by replacing it with a bridge.

Big changes were made at Grange. There was to be no wooden building on the platforms here. The bare Down platform gained a substantial shelter consisting of a pair of waiting rooms separated by a long screen wall with windows providing a view on to the Bay whilst protecting the platform from the wind. To further protect the passengers, glass and iron canopies, with a floral motif in the brackets, were erected over both platforms, giving the architecturally-complete range of buildings we know today. Agreement was made with the Brogdens for the road to Holme Island to be moved further

west and extended to Lindale. The railway needed to remove several level crossings. After some diplomatic correspondence with the new Grange Local Board, the station crossing was replaced by a subway whilst a pair of crossings between the new subway and Blawith Point were replaced by an elegant iron bridge. A second coal yard was made to the north of this bridge, connected by long sidings to the main yard.

Change in the passenger facilites at Carnforth did not occur until 1880 with the opening of the 'Furness & Midland Curve', allowing Midland Railway trains direct access into the joint station. The old train shed was removed, the platforms were extended and a bay provided for the Midland trains. Additional offices were provided, including a new

Carnforth. BR 7P 4-6-2 No. 70042 Lord Roberts pulls the 3-53 pm Manchester to Barrow train out of Carnforth station on 23 April 1955. The exchange sidings between the former Furness Railway and LNWR lines remained busy until after the end of steam. (CRA Photo Library ref. PEJ104)

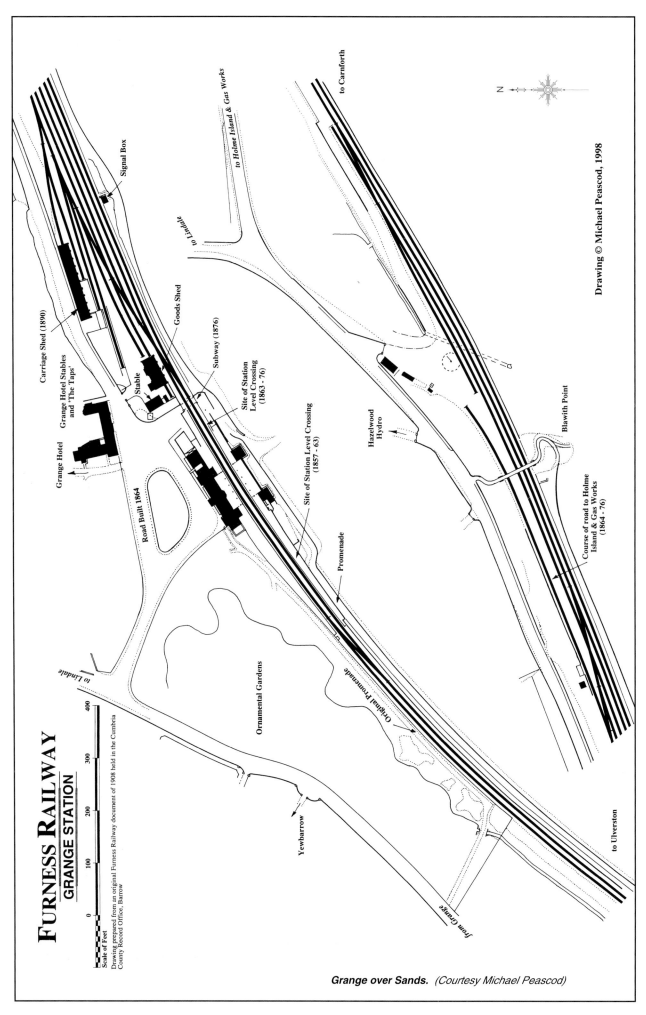

FURNESS RAILWAY
GRANGE STATION

Scale of Feet

0   100   200   300   400

Drawing prepared from an original Furness Railway document of 1908 held in the Cumbria County Record Office, Barrow

Drawing © Michael Peascod, 1998

Carriage Shed (1890)

Grange Hotel Stables and 'The Taps'

Signal Box

Stable

Goods Shed

Subway (1876)

Site of Station Level Crossing (1863 - 76)

Grange Hotel

Road Built 1864

Site of Station Level Crossing (1857 - 63)

to Holme Island & Gas Works

to Lindale

to Carnforth

Hazelwood Hydro

Blawith Point

Course of road to Holme Island & Gas Works (1864 - 76)

Promenade

Original Promenade

to Lindale

Ornamental Gardens

Yewbarrow

from Grange

to Ulverston

N

Grange over Sands. *(Courtesy Michael Peascod)*

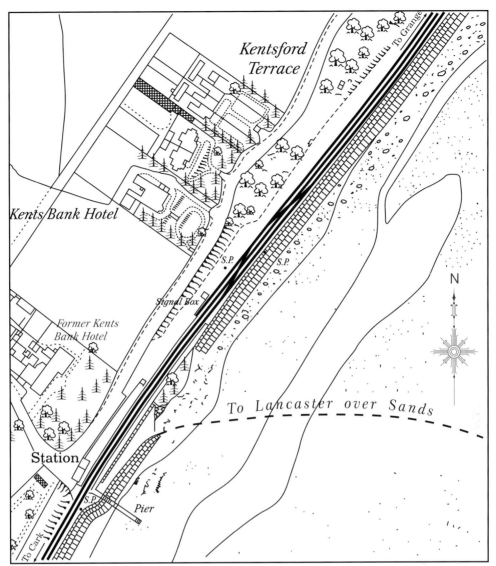

Kents Bank Station. *Drawing based on the Ordnance Survey map of 1891. The original Kents Bank Hotel stood against the old Cross-Bay road, running north west from the station. In later years a new establishment was set up amongst the villas just to the north east.*
(Drawn by Alan Johnstone, Crown Copyright Reserved)

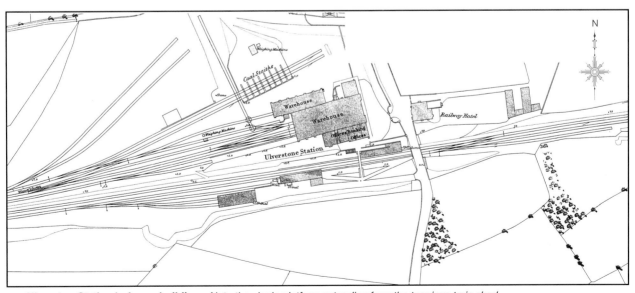

Ulverston Station before rebuilding. *Note the single platform extending from the terminus train shed.*
(From a microfilmed plan from the CRA Andrews Collection, Barrow CRO)

Kents Bank. *This view of circa 1890 shows the then new Up platform buildings beyond the original level crossing and station house dating probably from early FR days. Note the station bell to warn of the arrival of the train. The shelter on the right was built circa 1890 but replaced within five years by the present building at the north end of the Down platform.*
(Courtesy Grange over Sands Photographic Society, Dodgson Collection)

booking hall for FR and Midland patrons, topped off by a high glass roof. The F&M station near Warton was closed. By this time the Furness had a large locomotive shed and workshop west of the passenger station, and the goods yard off Warton Road, on the site of the FR's original loco facilities, had a large goods shed. Interchange sidings with the LNWR and Midland were everywhere!

Subsequent changes to the stations were more piecemeal. Kents Bank did not receive adequate station facilities until about 1890 when the station house lost its yard and a range of offices was built to the designs of (or in the style of) Paley & Austin. Having limestone walls to waist height with timber upper sections, the building included ticket office, porters room and toilet facilities. Change followed on the Down platform in 1895 when a new waiting shelter was built towards the northern end of the platform. Whilst its predecessor had been of wood and glass, the new building had limestone walls and an attractive red-tiled roof. The narrow platform was eventually widened to a uniform width in 1913, wooden decking being used to widen the narrow southern end.

At Arnside a new, more modern house was built in 1906 for the station master (Ulverston received one around the same time). The older cramped house became home to a platelayer. In 1910 the Up and Down platforms were extended to accommodate longer trains, with a footbridge between them. Until then access had been over the erstwhile level crossing. 1912 saw the widening of the bridge over Storth Road with the accompanying lowering of the road there. In 1914 the timber-framed building on the junction platform was replaced with the brick structure standing today.

At Grange the only noticable change for passengers was the provision, in 1909, of much needed lavatories on the Down platform. In fact facilities for the Kendal branch train had been improved much earlier. A carriage shed had been provided in 1890 at the back of the goods yard. The old tank house provided to water the branch

locomotive was replaced by a tank in the roof of the carriage shed, and a water column was erected alongside the siding used to stable the train between services. In 1900 a smart stable block, by Paley & Austin, was built near the goods shed

At Cark the Up platform buildings were altered around 1900 when access to the Gentlemen's lavatory was moved to a more discrete position. In 1907 the cattle landing on the Up side was extended and the layout of sidings was altered slightly. In the following year both platforms were raised and a footbridge was erected, slightly more ornate than others being put up along the FR at the time. In 1919 the then open booking hall and waiting area was enclosed by a wall closely matching the original Paley & Austin design.

The station had been known as Cark in Cartmel for most of its existence (the U&LR's option of Cark & Flookburgh never seems to have been formally adopted). This name was adopted by the Post Office for the village of Cark. In 1906 the Furness, presumably to show tourists that Cartmel was less than two easy miles away, subtly renamed the station Cark & Cartmel.

In 1911 a new halt was built at Wraysholme crossing, between Cark and Kents Bank, to serve the nearby Territorials' shooting range. Signals, controlled from a ground frame at the crossing house, protected the platforms and crossing. Although little used after the Great War, this was to survive into the early 1960s.

1916 saw the provision of a siding connecting the Up lay-by siding with the road into the Up goods yard, forming a loop for shunting off the main line, ostensibly for airship traffic. Some years earlier two sidings on the south side at Cark had been extended to hold 37 wagons each, in all probability to act as lay-by sidings for the increasing numbers of goods trains running to and from Barrow. For many years before and after, these sidings were also used to stable excursion trains bringing passengers for Cartmel Races. Cartmel Races had attracted excursions to Cark

Class 4F 0-6-0 No. 44317 *heads the 7-15 am Corkickle to St Helens goods train past Grange goods yard on 28 July 1958. Behind the loco is a pair of camping coaches. To the right stands the former carriage shed of 1890, erected to stable the 'Kendal Tommy' but made redundant by the 1930s. A water tank was under the raised pointed roof feeding the water column where the loco from 'Kendal Tommy' could be filled whilst the train stood in the sidings between services.* (CRA Photo Library ref. PEK382)

from the opening of the railway. Originally held on Whit Monday, with additional meetings added in 1947 on August Bank Holiday, the races drew thousands from the surrounding district. Most would then walk the mile and a half through the lanes to Cartmel, although into the 1970s Ribble Motor Services provided a special bus service between the villages.

Additional traffic appeared in 1927 when a wooden warehouse was built for the Furness & South Cumberland Supply Company of Broughton in Furness. This was located adjacent to the southernmost of the coal sidings in the Up side yard and remains, in much truncated form, today.

Modern architecture appeared on the U&LR lines in 1938 when the LMS demolished the 1880 train shed at Carnforth and adjacent canopies to allow the creation, for the first time, of a second, Down line, platform. The severe but then fashionable structure came into use from 3 July 1939.

The stations on the Ulverston & Lancaster section in 1964 were otherwise little changed from the 1900s. However, in that year the effects of Dr Richard Beeching's report on the future of British Railways started to be implemented. In March - April 1964 goods facilities were closed at Cark, Kents Bank, Arnside and Silverdale. Meathop siding closed at about the same time. Grange Gasworks ended production, with gas being supplied from the major gas facility at White Lund near Morecambe.

Grange goods yard was closed towards the end of May 1968, its business transferred to the still-open yard at Kendal. A change of a different kind occurred at Carnforth where the main line platforms were closed from 4 May 1970, leaving only awkward connections to the Morecambe – Leeds trains as a reason for changing trains there.

Station staffing was reduced to a minimum - a ticket clerk. At Carnforth, Grange and Ulverston the stations were manned by a ticket clerk and two porters on shifts. Further change came in May 1971 when conductor-guards were introduced between Lancaster and Barrow, and staffing at all but Grange and Ulverston became a thing of the past. An exception was at Cark where for some years in the 1970s a ticket clerk would be on duty on Cartmel Race days.

With many buildings now redundant, British Rail saw fit to demolish the Up side building at Cark in September 1986. This followed an attempt to let it for industrial use. Whilst there was interest, no-one was willing to take on the building in its run-down state. At Arnside the U&LR Down side buildings had been demolished in the previous July. In both cases smaller shelters were provided. Meanwhile, after time as a train crew signing-on point and then almost derelict, the buildings on the island platform at Carnforth have been transformed into a welcoming visitor centre with the refreshment room made famous in David Lean's film, Brief Encounter.

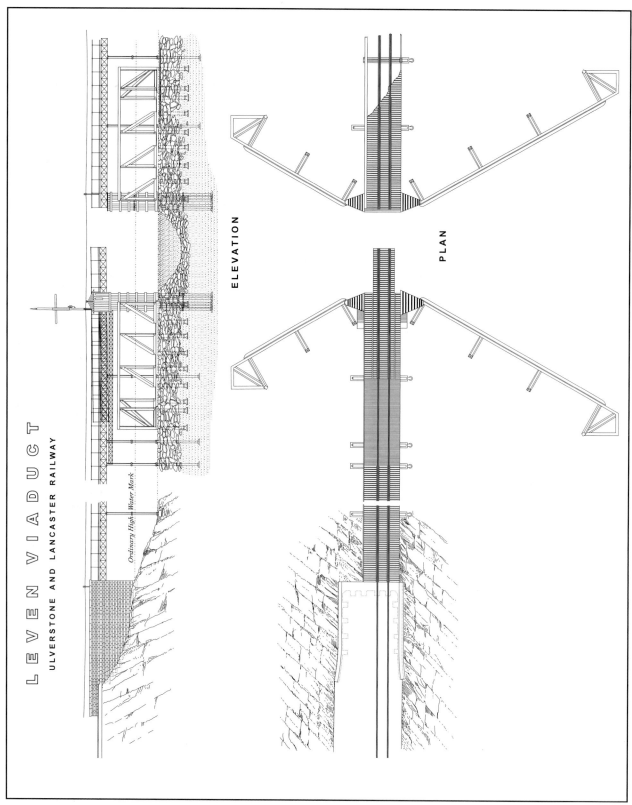

LEVEN VIADUCT

ULVERSTONE AND LANCASTER RAILWAY

ELEVATION

PLAN

Ordinary High Water Mark

The Kent and Leven viaducts of the U&LR *were admired by the engineering world of the time and drawings of them appeared in various publications. This contemporary plan and elevation show the arrangement of the opening span of the Leven viaduct. The fenders either side of the navigation channel are shown as built. The company had, however, originally agreed with the Admiralty that the fenders would run the full length of the seaward side of the viaduct.*

(Drawing by Alan Johnstone based on details from The Engineer*)*

The Viaducts

7

Arnside. *A view dating from about 1890 of the Kent Viaduct with Arnside beyond. This photograph by Gilbert Wilson of Grange shows just how slender and delicate the Kent and Leven viaducts were. Beyond the viaduct stands the resort of Arnside with the Crown Hotel on the left, previously called the Fighting Cocks and now named Ye Olde Fighting Cocks.* *(Author's Collection)*

THE EARLY UNSUCCESSFUL schemes for railways across Morecambe Bay saw no need for viaducts. Each was to tame the estuaries and divert the rivers into fixed canals or channels, easily crossed by a bridge. Whilst McClean & Stileman's plan for the Ulverstone & Lancaster Railway appears less ambitious on paper, their decision to use long viaducts show this was far from true.

It could be said that McClean & Stileman were a bit too ambitious because their proposal was for both Kent and Leven estuaries to be crossed on wooden viaducts, each some 737 yards long and with a 30 ft. opening bridge. This was some 50% longer than Brunlees decided to build, although he was to widen the navigable spans to 38 feet. Wooden viaducts were popular in Britain through the 19th century. The decision to adopt iron for the viaducts was heavily influenced by the shortage of Russian timber during the war in the Crimea, then under way. Another influence would have been John Brogden himself, following the purchase of the Tondu ironworks in Glamorgan (to give a market and showcase for its products). Brunlees, Henry Brogden and the contractor for the Leven Viaduct, Galloways of Manchester, must be given credit for the design and execution of the viaducts, such that when Messrs Featherstone obtained the contract for the Kent viaduct, all experimentation was complete and their task was relatively straightforward. Which of these suggested the design improvement for the drawbridge planned for the Kent isn't recorded.

These were pioneering structures through their use of cast and wrought iron in such a fine yet sturdy structure, capable of withstanding extremely powerful flows of water and winds whilst not having a solid foundation. Such a structure had to include an opening span to allow ships through, whilst being resilient to the exposure to wind and of relatively light weight: a lift bridge or swing bridge was out of the question. These structures would, 60 years later, carry the additional weight of brick and concrete casings around the piers and, 150 years after construction, a concrete deck.

The Leven was the first estuary to be crossed. The contractors were lucky that the first piles sunk into the sands, at the Ulverston end of the viaduct, had rock foundations, but within a few yards the rock fell away such that test bores of up to 70 feet failed to find a bottom to the sand and mud. This was far deeper than planned. The sand and mud would have to support the viaduct.

Brunlees had planned to use Mitchell screw piles, a relatively recent but well-established method and popular in offshore lighthouse construction at the time. At the other end of Morecambe Bay, off Fleetwood, such a lighthouse had been built in 1839-40. Brunlees was taken aback by the high cost of licences to use this patented method. To get around this he, with Brogden and Galloway, developed a method of sinking the piles using a jet of water. Several designs of pile were tried before they achieved success. The successful design took advantage of the hollow cast iron pile, to which a 2 foot 6 inch diameter disk was fixed on the bottom. In the centre of the disk was a hole of 2 or 3 inches diameter. Rather than hammer or screw the piles down, a tube was placed through the hole in the base of the pile through which water was passed at pressure. The combination of agitating the pile in one direction then the other, plus the force of the water disturbing the sand and mud below, allowed the pile to sink under its own weight until it held firm.

There was a great deal of trial and error until the method was perfected. Work commenced in June 1855. On 30 November 1855 a trial pile was still under test: it was weighted with 10 tons of iron and sank $4^{3}/_{4}$ inches. On 21 January 1856 another trial pile was weighted with 20 tons; it sank half an inch, but then on 13 February Mr Kerr was noted to have weighted one with 20 tons and it sank $2^{3}/_{4}$ inches. Progress was not helped by the conditions of having to work in a tidal river channel. On 21 January 1856 Galloway's punt used for driving the piles sank and the pumping engine was upturned into the sands! But by March 1856 the trials were over, the method perfected and permanent piles were sunk.

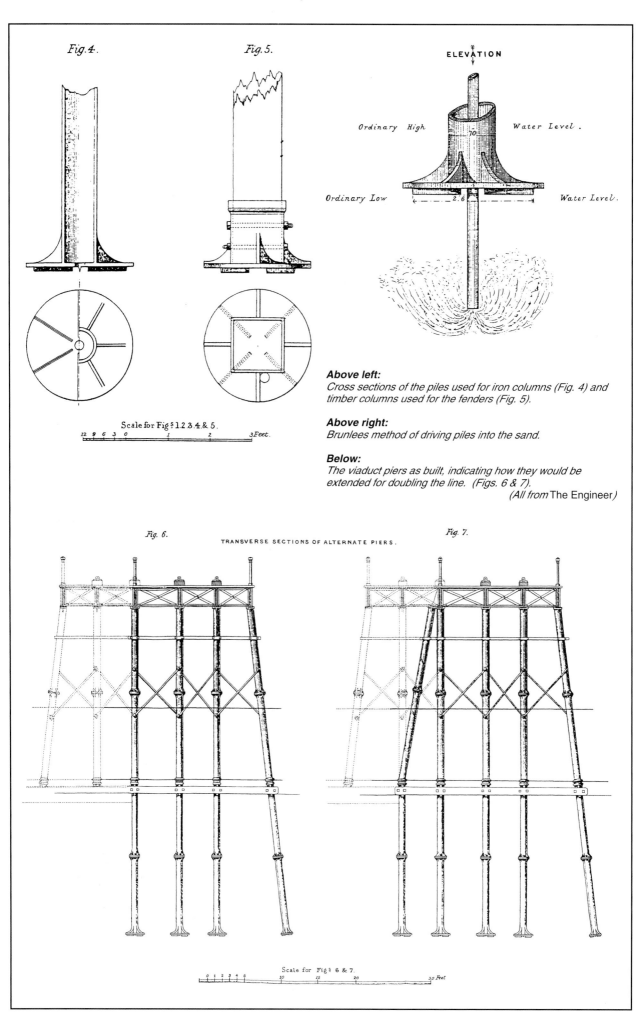

Fig.4.   Fig.5.   ELEVATION

Ordinary High   Water Level.

Ordinary Low   Water Level.

Scale for Figs 1.2.3.4.& 5.

Above left:
Cross sections of the piles used for iron columns (Fig. 4) and timber columns used for the fenders (Fig. 5).

Above right:
Brunlees method of driving piles into the sand.

Below:
The viaduct piers as built, indicating how they would be extended for doubling the line. (Figs. 6 & 7).
(All from The Engineer)

Fig. 6.   TRANSVERSE SECTIONS OF ALTERNATE PIERS.   Fig. 7.

Scale for Figs 6 & 7.

Construction of both viaducts was then similar. The structure built onto the piles originally consisted of piers spaced to give approximately 30 foot spans. Each pier was made up of cast iron columns. Three were vertical and, on the seaward side, there was a raked column to provide additional strength and resistance against the tides and anything that may be floating therein! On the inland side on alternate piers were raked columns, hinged at the pile so that when the viaduct was widened to allow double track they would be brought to the vertical and only a further solid raked pile would be needed. The track was carried on wrought iron girders seated on the vertical columns. The raked columns carried further girders to carry the timber decking. The exception was the section at the opening span, as will become clear. Most components were sourced from Galloways' own works in Manchester together with some from Brogden's own ironworks at Tondu. Prefabrication took place at a foundry set up alongside Ulverston Canal before the parts were taken to the construction site.

As the piles and columns were in place, they were protected from scouring by a weir of stones, laid just above the level of the sands, except for the gap for the navigable channel. This would be a bone of contention with many having an interest in the estuaries, who saw this as a further restriction on the channels. The channel was so restricted only at low tide when it would be fairly narrow anyway. The tides soon passed over the height of the stones and for most periods during a tide they were covered and the flows in either direction could utilise the full width of the viaducts.

The principal of the opening span was a counterbalanced platform, which extended over the navigation channel in the one direction (a gap of 38 feet) and a similar distance in the other. When the platform was withdrawn, it would rise on the channel side with the other side below the adjacent girders of the viaduct. The platform then rolled back to leave the necessary gap. On the Leven viaduct this movable platform was on wheels, running on a track sloping back under the viaduct between the piers. Windlasses placed either side of the 'dropping' section of platform released a cam that allowed the platform to drop. The bridgemaster would then go to the pivot and by turning a wheel withdraw

the platform. The platform was returned to the closed position by reversing this process. An article in The Engineer claimed a man and a boy could work the bridge.

Signals were erected at the drawbridge. A pair of arms faced both upstream and downstream to indicate to shipmasters that the bridge was withdrawn and passage available. On the same post a pair of arms protected the railway. Distant signals were also provided on the railway at the requisite distance in either direction.

The Kent drawbridge, if it was ever installed, was to be an advance on that over the Leven, resulting in a lighter structure. Instead of the platform having wheels, the lower face of the girders acted as a sled running on wheels attached to the adjacent piers. Control would have been similar to the Leven drawbridge.

At the start of 1863 the Furness Railway Company were planning the completion of work to double what was now the Ulverston to Carnforth section of their railway. Ulverston to the Leven viaduct had been doubled in 1860 and the section east of the viaduct to Cark in the following year. Messrs Galloway won the contract to widen both viaducts to allow for double track and to replace the wooden decking with wrought iron plates for a total of £16,500. Work was started on the Leven viaduct around 21 March. The planned completion date was the end of August. At the beginning of that month Galloways had completed all but the opening span in doubling the Leven viaduct. It would be November before the viaducts were ready.

Whether Galloways were cutting corners or had the agreement of McClean & Stileman, the foundations for the new vertical and raking piles differed from their predecessors. Rather than sinking the piles deep into the sand, they were instead rested on large stone blocks of four feet square and 18 inches deep and covered by the widened weir of stones! Surprisingly these foundations were found to be in excellent condition when the viaducts were rebuilt in 1913-17.

The FR were authorised to stop using the drawbridge on the Leven viaduct in their Act of 1866, which also authorised the Newby Bridge branch and Canal branch. The Bridge Register, recording the passage of vessels through

***A 1930s view from the Leven viaduct**, looking towards Leven Junction and Plumpton Junction. The gentleman is standing in the walkway provided to allow foot passage at low tide over the western river channel (added by the LMS). At the end of the viaduct stands the pair of ex-U&LR cottages. The building on the down side was at various times a smithy, used in repairs to the original viaduct, and a temporary signal box during the various re-decking and rebuilding exercises in FR days. The wind-pressure recorder can be seen to the left of this building, with the tall junction home signals and Leven Junction signal box beyond.*
(CRA Photo Library ref. PA0046)

The Leven Viaduct Wind Pressure Gauge. *Mounted on a fine sandstone plinth, the pressure gauge was disused by the time this photograph was taken in the late 1970s. A pocket notebook has been placed alongside to indicate its size. By this time the southern pressure plate had fallen off and much of the recording mechanism removed. (Author)*

the navigation channel, was last used at the viaduct in 1865. It was then used to record vessels passing through the lock of Ulverston Canal. The bridgemaster also served as lock-keeper and appears to have been based, according to contemporary newspaper reports, at Canal Foot. Vessels were certainly still sailing up to Greenodd in March 1867. In fact vessels were sailing to the Lowwood Gunpowder Company's wharf at Roudsea Powder Magazines as late as 1879, when that company were considering building a long pier out into the estuary. Their vessel was, at that time, capable of passing under the viaduct without need of a drawbridge. Presumably it was either a steamer or capable of lowering its masts. The signals at the drawbridge were still operational in May 1869 when the Newby Bridge branch was inspected for the Board of Trade. Colonel Hutchinson observed that the signals at Leven Junction signal box should be interlocked with those on the viaduct.

The drawbridge wasn't actually removed for another 17 years. In 1884 Frank Stileman, the FR Consultant Engineer, indicated that it was necessary to replace the main girders on the Kent and Leven viaducts. That October Messrs Andrew Handyside & Company won the contract to replace the girders and decking. The work was carried out without closing the line. Instead single line working was adopted over each viaduct as work was under way. Single line working over the Kent viaduct was in operation from 31 May to 7 December 1885, controlled from Arnside signal box at the east end and a temporary box, 'Kent Viaduct', at the western end. The process was repeated on the Leven viaduct with Single Line Working in operation between 2 May and 15 November 1886. This was controlled from a temporary signal box installed at the eastern end of the viaduct named 'Leven Viaduct', with Leven Junction box controlling the west end.

The viaducts proved to be remarkably strong and resisted the actions of the tides and the winds admirably. The same could not be said for wooden railway carriages. On the night of 26 February 1903 a heavy storm hit most of the western coast of France and Britain. Heavy waves and strong winds blew ships aground: the wind rushing into Morecambe Bay was no exception. Wind or no wind, the first passenger train from Carnforth on 27 February, the 4-25 am Down Mail train had to run. Thomas Shaw braved the elements to get his train of 12 vans and carriages towards Furness.

Driver Shaw and his fireman, Harry Barker, with 4-4-0 loco No. 22 at the head of the train, left Carnforth 9 minutes late. All was well on the inland section of the line, but after the train passed Arnside the wind blew the telegraph wires down on the exposed embankment between the Kent Viaduct and Meathop. The train stopped to clear the wires, which had broken the headcode lamp, and then proceeded on to Grange. The wires were down between there and Cark too. Following rules, Shaw was given a caution ticket to be given up at Cark. Signalman Tingey recorded that the Mail Train left Cark at 5-25 am, and that he still had telegraphic communication with Plumpton Junction, the next signal box open at that time of the morning. The train had then to pass over the exposed embankments out onto the Leven viaduct.

The train hit fallen wires on the Capeshead embankment around 300 yards before the viaduct but it appeared no damage was done. The train continued only to be brought to a stand on the viaduct. The brakes had come on with the loco just short of the old opening span. Winds of over 100 mph were blowing up the Leven estuary with gusts up to 120 mph. Poor Harry Barker had the job of looking for the problem. He found a wire wrapped around a brake pipe, thus applying the brakes. He removed this and returned to No. 22. The visibility in the storm was bad, but not so bad as to prevent him from seeing two vans blow over onto the Up line. He couldn't see what had happened to the rest of the train but the guards, postal staff and passengers knew that all but the FR mail van closest to the engine were on their sides.

Barker made his way slowly towards Plumpton Junction and Guard Isaac Holmes went to lay detonators to protect the train from the east. Barker was picked up by the bank engine, sent by the Plumpton signalman to find the missing mail train, and taken to that signalbox. Meanwhile Shaw, Holmes and Guard Kelly helped the passengers and postal staff from the train and across the viaduct to the railway cottages at the end of the viaduct. They must have been petrified, with gales blowing, waves lapping the deck of the viaduct and their train having nearly been blown into the sea.

The Plumpton Junction signalman, Job Miller, raised the alarm and by 6-30 am Doctors Bowman and Carter from Ulverston had arrived with railway officials and staff. Although all the travellers were by now in the safety of the platelayers' cottages, Bowman led a search party onto the viaduct to check no-one had been left behind.

The breakdown gangs arrived by 7-20 am from Barrow and Carnforth. The mail van was rerailed followed by the remaining carriages. The mails were recovered and sent on their way by special train. The storm had abated

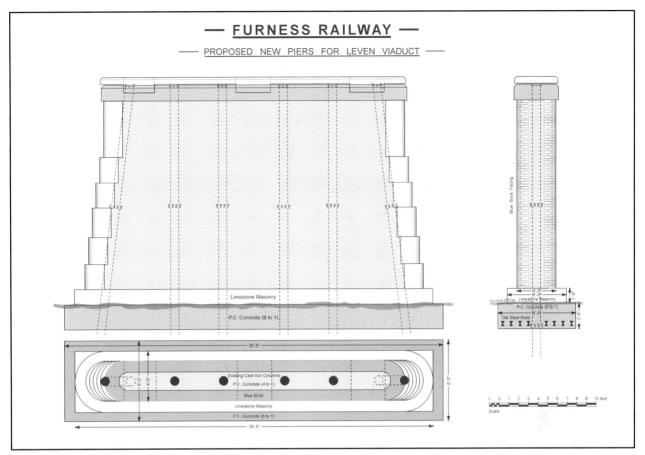

Cross-sections of the piers on the Leven Viaduct, *showing how the original piers were encased in brick and concrete. The Kent viaduct piers were similarly dealt with.*

(Drawing by Alan Johnstone based on a document in Barrow CRO)

somewhat by now and the carriages and vans were put back onto the track and taken away. No damage was done to either locomotive or the viaduct and the line was reopened by 4-30 pm that afternoon.

Following the inevitable Board of Trade inquiry, Major Druitt recommended that either a high parapet be placed on the Leven viaduct to protect the trains from high winds or a wind pressure gauge be installed. The Board's recommendations were only that. They had no powers to force the FR to follow the recommendations, but at the same time the railway company knew it would be in trouble should this occur again. Whilst a high parapet was impractical in such an exposed location, a wind pressure gauge was duly obtained. This was placed on a sandstone plinth at Tridley Point, close to the west end of the viaduct. It was connected electrically to the signal boxes at Plumpton Junction and Cark. Should a wind of 32 lbs pressure be measured, alarm bells would ring in these signal boxes and trains thus prevented from crossing the viaduct. The Wind Gauge also included a paper recorder. The signalling department electrician inspected the device weekly into the 1970s, when it fell into disuse. Several years after the author observed the remains of the gauge, around 1980, an anemometer was erected at the western end of the Capeshead embankment, again connected to Plumpton Junction signal box. This continued in operation until the closure of Plumpton Junction box when the anemometer was deemed unnecessary. Now the signallers at Arnside, Grange and Ulverston receive warnings of high winds from meteorological sources and suitable precautions taken, often including the closure of the line until the storm has passed.

During 1907 the Furness railway engineers began to have concerns over the state of the viaducts and carried out some estimates for reconstruction. The Board deferred any action for twelve months. The following year Frank Stileman again reported on the viaducts. This time the Board authorised some strengthening work. However, only a

limited amount of essential maintenance could be done. In both years the Furness Railway had been in financial difficulties, with no dividend declared in 1907. In 1913 the new FR Engineer, David Rutherford, reported his concerns over the state of the viaducts and put forward proposals for rebuilding work. The sums necessary were great. As with companies even today, the consultants were called in to justify the expenditure. Messrs Rendal, Palmer and Tritton were approached to verify Rutherford's reports and consider deferring any work. The consultant engineers inspected the Leven viaduct in May and June 1913 and promptly presented a dismal report. Not only were the columns cracked and often repaired with steel sleeves, but below the level of the stone weir, now consolidated after 56 years into a quite solid foundation, the cast iron was so soft and degraded that there was little iron left in the structure. It was possible to hammer nails into the metal! The Kent viaduct was in a better state, but only just. The 1885-6 re-decking hadn't helped matters. Rather than each span having separate girders capable of independent expansion, Handysides had riveted the new girders together such that they were continuous for the full length of the viaduct. Consequently the piers at the ends of the viaducts were slowly rocked whenever heat or cold expanded and contracted the girders.

Given most of the girders on the viaducts were sound, the most cost-effective solution was to encase the old piers with brick and concrete on a concrete foundation just below the level of the stone weir. On the Kent viaduct the inner piers of the double piers adjacent to the navigable channel were removed, as were the piers whose primary purpose had been to carry the ends of the drawbridge when withdrawn (still in place but redundant since 1885). On the Leven viaduct the opportunity was taken to widen the main channel, and new piers were built adjacent to the old double piers, giving a clear span of 60 feet. New steel girders were installed to bridge these longer spans.

As in 1885-6, single line working was introduced over each viaduct as work was carried out. A temporary signal box, 'Leven East', was installed in an old carriage body at the east end of the Leven viaduct with a further temporary signal box, 'Leven West', installed in the maintenance shed and smithy at the west end. Single Line working was in operation between 24 August 1913 and 24 April 1915. Whilst the work was under way the resident engineer, James Alexander carried out experiments on ways to cause the concrete to set quickly. This was necessitated by the twice-daily tides passing under the viaduct and over the new foundations.

Once the Leven viaduct was completed, the engineering team moved their attentions to the Kent viaduct. Again single line working was needed and a temporary signal box again erected at the west end of the viaduct. This time it was named 'Arnside West'. Single Line working was in operation between 9 May 1915 and 6 October 1917.

As will have been noted, the works were undertaken largely during the Great War. As a result, the cost of rebuilding exceeded the original estimates. During the period bricks, concrete, steel and labour had all increased in price.

As mentioned several times, the silting up of the canal lock gates and later of North Lonsdale Ironworks' piers just to the south, was always blamed on the Leven viaduct. During the 1913 – 1915 rebuilding, two 3-foot-diameter pipes had been embedded into the weir under the viaduct beneath one of the western spans in an attempt to increase the flow through the viaduct at low tide. In 1927 both the Ulverston Urban District Council and the North Lonsdale Ironworks company argued for a second channel through the weir. The LMS acceded to their wishes in an agreement dated 4 March 1927.

During the early 1990s British Rail found themselves in the position whereby the Leven and Kent viaducts needed significant maintenance. Money was tight and the investment was kept to a minimum: painting the ironwork and replacing the timberwork bearing the track. The work was mainly focussed on one line, on the basis that at least the line over each viaduct could be singled should their condition get worse. The Kent viaduct was dealt with over an 8-week period during late 1990 with the Leven viaduct being dealt with the following March.

The new century has seen interesting changes in attitudes towards railways following privatisation and the subsequent quasi-nationalisation of the rail infrastructure under Network Rail. Thus in 2005 a full structural survey was carried out on the Leven Viaduct. Corrosion found on the main girders, decking and walkways showed that it again needed major investment. The prime contractors for the work, Carillion Rail, had the advantage of a complete closure of the line from Grange to Barrow in which to complete their work, with passengers being bussed between stations. The work was undertaken between 26 March and 16 July 2006 at a cost of £1.4 million.

The task undertaken by Network Rail was equally as great as the two earlier rebuilding schemes. The brick piers were repointed and all but the 65-foot girders were replaced by concrete decking, prefabricated by Messrs Fairfield Mabey of Chepstow. Network Rail quote 3,500 tonnes of steelwork as being removed. Whilst the track-bearing girders dated from 1886, the outer walkway girders were probably those of 1857–63. The old girders went to Cark for removal by road and new walkways brought to site from there. The new walkways also served to act as support for the gantries used in replacing the main decking. The old decks were removed via Ulverston goods yard from where the new decks were delivered. The 65-foot girders of 1913 were thoroughly grit-blasted and repainted. Trusses were fitted beneath to connect the concrete decks on either side and allow for movement due to temperature or braking forces of trains.

Whilst this work was under way a new subway was installed at Grange, in theory to replace nearby Bailey Lane crossing. The two footbridges, at Clare House and beside the old swimming pool were also removed, although the former may be replaced.

Thus the Ulverstone & Lancaster Railway is in a fit state for the twenty-first century.

Ulverston, its Environs & Industries

8

THE BROGDEN'S PRIME objective for the Ulverstone & Lancaster Railway had been to ship ore to South Staffordshire, to the ironworks of the Black Country. Even when the Furness Railway had bailed the company out of its financial difficulties, there was no significant change to this objective. As a result, Ulverston had found itself with rail connections to the rest of Britain but with little encouragement to trade by rail, the only sidings being at the old station above the town and isolated from the industries. The canal, although in Brogden and subsequently Furness Railway hands, and despite early hopes by the townsfolk, remained isolated: communications to and from the canal were purely by road.

A series of apparently unconnected events led to the development of new industries alongside the canal and south towards Conishead Priory: the Furness Railway's desire to close the opening span of the Leven viaduct, their need for an easier route to Barrow, the opening of the North Lonsdale ironworks and the acquisition of the Conishead Priory estate by property developers.

The first event followed the purchase of the U&LR by the Furness. As described earlier, the opening span of the Leven viaduct was as much a hindrance to the railway as it was an awkward help to prolonging the life of the port of Greenodd. Ships had difficulty negotiating the opening, with subsequent damage to the viaduct and claims for recompense by the ship-owners. The need to open the span either side of high tide also hindered the passage of trains. The Furness saw the closure of this hindrance as something to be pursued, and in 1863 approached the wharf-owners and ship-owners to gain agreement to this. These were an influential group, led by John Barraclough Fell, the engineer and long-time wharf owner at Greenodd. Their solicitor was John Poole, whom we shall meet again. The resultant agreement was to the effect that, if the FR provided a rail link to Greenodd and to the Canal, with special rates for goods between the two places, the affected parties would not object to the bridge being closed to navigation. There can't have been any rush on the part of the Furness since nothing immediately happened.

Two years later the FR Directors were in Derby meeting their counterparts at the Midland Railway headquarters. A result of that meeting was the revival of the branch line to Newby Bridge to connect with the Windermere steamers. This would meet their obligation to serve Greenodd whilst generating tourist traffic from West Yorkshire via the Furness & Midland joint line from Carnforth. The branch, among other things, was authorized by Parliament in the FR Act authorized in the 1865-6 session. This also ratified a further Greenodd Navigation agreement, with its special tariffs on goods between Greenodd and Ulverston Canal or Barrow for onward shipping, and authorized a siding to serve the new basin on the Canal.

Construction of the Newby Bridge branch took three years, with the line opened to Greenodd for goods traffic in March 1869. The station and branch were built across the wharves at Greenodd. The remainder of the branch, beyond Newby Bridge to the new wharf at Lakeside, opened through the spring and summer of that year. The Greenodd wharf-owners and ship-owners committee met several times with the Furness company, and in December 1869 confirmed their agreement with the FR to close the opening span and effectively close the port. The opening span was closed, and any ships continuing to trade had to lower their masts to get through the navigable channel – possibly a more dangerous act than when the span opened.

Whilst goods could get to and from Greenodd by rail, they couldn't get by rail to and from the canal. It wasn't until 1869 that the contract plans for the canal siding were drawn up. The siding, 33 chains in length, was to leave the FR main line just west of the Canal Viaduct, falling steeply down to the level of the towpath, and running as far as the slagheap of the erstwhile Low Furness Ironworks. A siding then ran back alongside the new basin. It must be recalled that the main railway at this point is climbing at a gradient of 1 in 82 - steep by any standards. The siding fell at an even steeper gradient – 1 in 74 initially and rising to 1in 50 before it reached the canal side. One must admire the courage of the railway men who worked the trains down to the canal and managed to get them back up to the main line!

Construction appears to have occurred with the completion of works on the Newby Bridge branch in late 1869, after opening to passengers. It was 1870 before the merchants of Greenodd could transport their wares by rail between the new basin on Ulverston Canal and their village. The industries at the canal head however remained isolated from the railway. One unique load was sourced from the Canal branch. During the early 1870s, John Fell, of Ulverston, was secretly building a yacht, to be called the *Char*, in the old ironworks buildings. His plan was to race the *Char* on Windermere in competition to the *Britannia* owned by Major Ridealgh of Fell Foot. Unfortunately its builder, Foreman Shipbuilder William Beck, was killed when the vessel was taken on a railway wagon from the canal siding to Lakeside on 7 May 1873. The tender for the yacht was carried on a barrier wagon between the locomotive and that carrying the yacht. Beck was travelling in the smaller vessel; when it passed through Ulverston passenger station he somehow lost his footing, fell between the moving wagons and was fatally injured.

The second event influencing the construction of railways in Ulverston was as a result of the profitability of the Furness Railway Company combined with thoughts of an easier route from Lindal to Barrow Ironworks. This was to be in two adjacent sections: the Gleaston Loop from Lindal to Salthouse Junction, Barrow; and the Barrow Loop from Salthouse Junction to Cocken, just north of the ironworks on the existing Hawcoat Branch. A bill for both lines was submitted in 1871 but before the bill had completed its passage through Parliament, the company withdrew the Gleaston Loop, save for the associated branch line to the haematite mines at and around Stank. In its place the company considered a longer, easier line from Salthouse, around the coast to Plumpton Junction: the Bardsea Loop. This line appears to have been in active preparation in 1874. The northern section, from Plumpton Junction to Bardsea, was authorized by the Furness Railway Act 1876, together with the Park Loop from Cocken to the existing Furness line to Kirkby, Millom and Whitehaven near to Park Ore Depot. By this time the Furness, together with other Barrow industries, were facing a drop in profits, leading the company to reconsider its ambitions, restricting these to enhancing its existing station facilities and, perhaps misguidedly in retrospect, continuing to develop Barrow Docks. The seed was sown, however.

Event number three occurred in 1873. With the continued growth in the demand for iron by industry, the owners of various haematite mines in Furness, primarily the Kennedy family and Messrs Harrison Ainslie, decided to build their own modern ironworks. They formed the North Lonsdale Iron & Steel Company Limited, incorporated in October that year. The chosen site for the new works was on the banks of Ulverston Canal, some way south of the

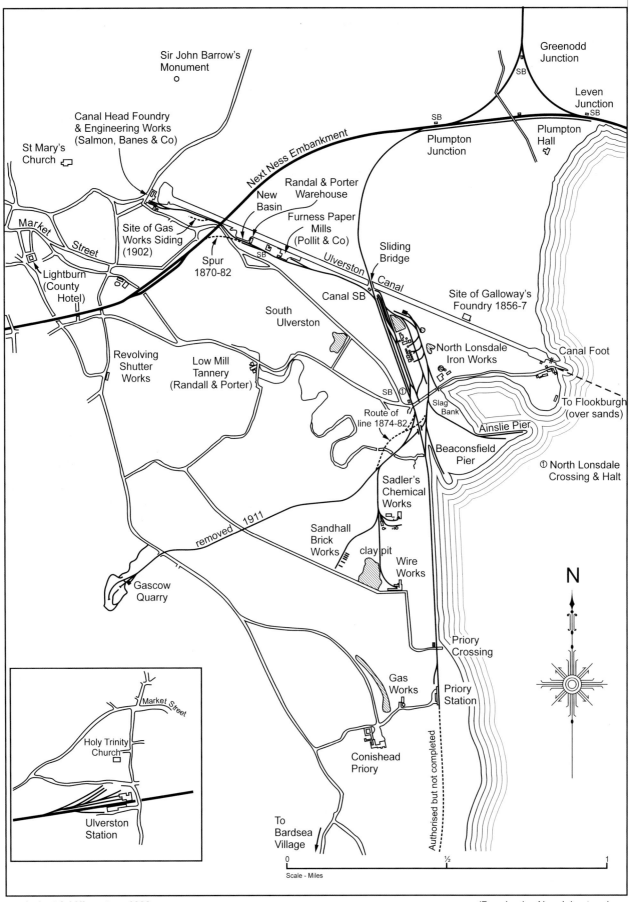

Industrial Ulverston, 1890.   *(Drawing by Alan Johnstone)*

Furness main line and the canal siding, but adjacent to, and aligned with, the course of the possible Bardsea Loop. Presumably FR Managing Director James Ramsden and NLI&SCo's founders discussed their respective schemes.

The new ironworks were built during 1874, with the first furnace going into blast on 5 May 1876. Six furnaces were envisaged but only four were built, the final furnace going into blast in 1879. Rail access was required to the new works. The immediate solution was to extend the existing canal siding along the south bank of the canal to the ironworks. No parliamentary authority was immediately sought since the line was built on railway-owned property. The work was carried out by Barrow contractor William Gradwell. It is probable that a siding was provided north from the new basin to Messrs Salmon, Barnes' Canal Head Foundry at that time. At the same time, another new industry established itself on the banks of the canal. The Furness Paper Mills set up their works between the new basin and the North Lonsdale ironworks, on the site of the erstwhile Low Furness Ironworks. Sidings were provided for the paper mill.

The fourth event influencing how the railways developed in the area under discussion had its origins earlier in the century. In the early years of the 19th century, Conishead Priory was the seat of the Braddyll family. The Braddylls were owners of many coal mines in County Durham, including the South Hetton Coal Company, and had become rich from the profits. These profits were invested in their home and its valuable collection of furniture and paintings. The Priory developed into a fantastic mock-gothic mansion, initially to the designs of fashionable architect Philip Wyatt and completed by the Kendal architect George Webster. With their money thus tied up, it must come as no surprise that, following several years of financial difficulties, T R G Braddyll ran out of money, the means to continue his family's lavish lifestyle. Bankruptcy followed in 1848 and Conishead Priory was auctioned in 1852. The buyers, through Ulverston solicitors Petty and Postlethwaite, were a group of cousins, often referred to as the Heirs of Christopher Rawlinson. Rawlinson was a long deceased landowner from Cark whose estate still remained undivided by his heirs. The new occupant was H W Askew. Askew and his cousins unsuccessfully tried to sell the property in 1864, renting it out to mining magnate H W Schneider for a time. It was to be July 1874 before he, or rather the Heirs, managed to dispose of the property.

The new owners were a group of local men described by neighbour Captain Henry Gale of Bardsea Hall as 'speculative gentlemen'. The prime mover was local solicitor John Poole, in partnership with contractor William Gradwell and Civil Engineer A H Strongitharm. Poole was Clerk to the Ulverston Local Board, amongst other things, whilst Strongitharm was a partner of Edward Wadham, civil engineer and local agent to the Duke of Buccleuch. Strongitharm's other claim to fame was as engineer to the Rowrah & Kelton Fell Mineral Railway in West Cumberland. Gradwell had been involved in the development of Barrow-in-Furness since the early 1850s when he imported timber through that port. He had built many of the buildings in the town and extended his operations into general contracting. Both Gradwell and Strongitharm were members of Barrow Borough Council, each serving a term as Mayor.

Almost straight away Gradwell took advantage of his investment at Conishead Priory, opening up a quarry at Gascow Farm in partnership with James Bush. Gradwell and Bush contracted to supply Gascow limestone to the new North Lonsdale Ironworks. They built a standard gauge tramway from the ironworks, across the fields of their new property, across the Bardsea road and into the quarry. Locomotives were employed on the work straight away, as witnessed by a complaint proposed to be raised by Captain Gale to the Lancashire Assizes of January 1877. His issue was that Gradwell had been allowed to build his tramway across the Bardsea road, without

necessary legal authority and only on the say-so of John Poole, partner in the estate and clerk to the Local Board. A further gripe was that the rails were above the level of that road. On the plus side, we do learn from Gale's submission that Gradwell employed a man to watch the crossing and that gates were provided.

In October 1876 the Conishead Priory estate had been split, with Gradwell and Strongitharm retaining much of the land between the Priory grounds and the new ironworks and between the sea and west to beyond the Bardsea road. Thus they retained Gascow Quarry and the long-established estate brick works. The latter had been usually let by the estate to independent brick makers and used for the production of drainage tiles, among other things. Gradwell brought it under his own control, under the title of the Ulverston Brick Making Company. Gradwell and Strongitharm's idea was to develop their new property as an up-market housing estate. In the area to the east of the Ulverston road, excepting a few plots occupied by the brick works and a new chemical works, to be described, each field was to become the site of a villa, whilst the small area west of the Bardsea road and adjacent to Gascow Quarry was divided up into a number of smaller development plots.

This potential development of an exclusive estate of villas was the fourth event to influence the railways in the area. Gradwell and Ramsden's plans were interdependent. Even before the new railway was authorised, Ramsden, Gradwell and Poole had entered into an agreement that the railway could purchase land from the Priory estate whilst in return all but express trains would stop at a station on the estate. Gradwell needed the new railway, not only to serve the new estate but also to protect it from the sea! Those who know the area will know that this low-lying land is former salt marsh and not much above the level of high tide. Consequently, whilst normally well drained, after prolonged heavy rain the water table thereabouts can rise and cause flooding.

The chemical works mentioned above were established by the North Yorkshire industrialist S A Sadler. Opened in July 1876, the firm refined pitch and other tar products. It is assumed that the site chosen, at Sand Hall, was to allow Sadler to move tar from his major coke ovens in North Yorkshire with the trains of coke being supplied to the North Lonsdale ironworks. Presumably the daily trainload of coke ensured the timely transportation of tar to this remote outpost of the Sadler empire. The works were built between the ironworks site and Conishead Priory, and served from the outset by a siding off Gradwell's tramway. The firm employed its own locomotive to shunt the works.

With the new industries and the potential for first-class passenger traffic, the Furness Railway proceeded to gain authority for the northern section of the Bardsea loop. Authorized in the Furness Railway Act, 1876, it was to run just over two miles from Plumpton Junction, past the North Lonsdale ironworks and on along the shore, cutting through the edge of the grounds of Conishead Priory, to the shore below Bardsea village. The section from Salthouse to Bardsea had been omitted from the Bill.

With the prospect of a railway to serve Bardsea, the Conishead Hydropathic Company was formed. This was incorporated in 1878 to convert the mansion into a grand hotel with accommodation for 150 guests (and the potential for 240). The Hydropathic company timed the conversion and subsequent opening of the 'Hydro' with the expected opening of the branch to passengers. The Furness guarantee to stop all but express passenger trains at the Priory now applied to the Hydro.

The route of the new line was that of a main line railway with light gradients and no sharp curves. Gradwell obtained the contract to build the line. With the financial stringency then in force, the Furness reconsidered building the line all the way to Barrow. The line was double track throughout but stopped short of the authorized Bardsea terminus. The end of the line was at a station in the grounds of Conishead Priory, appropriately named Priory. Land was acquired only

***North Lonsdale Crossing
signal box in the 1950s.*** *An
ex MR 2F 0-6-0 stands at the
then limit of the branch, just
before the site of the
crossing.
(CRA Photo Library
ref. JA1119)*

up to Red Lane (named from the colour of the road due to haematite being carted from the Lindal mines to Morecambe Bay at the historic loading point of Conishead Bank) and a certain amount of construction was started: today an isolated bridge stands forlorn in the middle of a field along with some of the fencing erected to mark the limits of railway land. The contractors' depot during construction was in Gascow Quarry, from where much construction material was also obtained.

Construction of the line was slow. In fact there was little reason to rush. As mentioned earlier, the Furness Railway Company and most Barrow industries were experiencing a trade depression. Investment into its new Ramsden and Cavendish Docks and into stations up and down their system continued, but these too were done at a slower rate. The new industries alongside the canal and on the Conishead estate were served by the Canal branch (for it was no longer just a siding). However the daily goods train had to be shunted first at Plumpton Junction, since the branch was only accessed from a trailing point on the Down (Barrow) line and then manoeuvred down the 1 in 50 gradient to the Canal Sidings. Whilst this would have been difficult to work when a few wagons to and from the Newby Bridge branch were being shunted, it must have been a sight to see a train of coke, coal and iron ore being shunted down and the empty wagons or loads of pig iron being raised to the main line!

Most of the construction was completed by 1881 and in that summer the Executors of William Gradwell sold off a significant amount of construction equipment. All that remained was the canal bridge, which Gradwell's built from parts supplied by Westray & Copeland of Barrow. Ulverston Canal signal box opened at the end of July 1882. As this box controlled the canal bridge, it must mark the date from which the FR diverted goods traffic for the Canal and South Ulverston industries over the new line.

In 1880, the FR applied to Parliament to, among other things, retrospectively authorize the Canal branch from the Canal basin to Ulverston Canal signal box. The Furness Railway Act, 1881, as it became, also allowed for the closure of the spur from the main line down to the new basin once the link from the Canal branch to the Bardsea branch was completed and traffic could reach the basin via the new line. Tolls under the Greenodd Navigation agreements of 1869 were to apply to the new route. Rights of way along the

south-eastern tow-path were also rescinded. At an unknown date, but probably soon after the opening of the Bardsea branch to goods and mineral traffic, the connection from the main line at the canal viaduct down to the Canal branch was removed. Other aspects of the 1881 Act affecting Ulverston were permission to divert a road at the canal head and alterations to previous obligations regarding water in the canal. In the 1852 Ulverston Waterworks Act (see Chapter 3), the Water Company was obliged to supply a certain volume of water into the canal. The FR now wanted to charge the NLI&SCo. for water it was using in its works. Ulverston Local Board, as successors of the Water Company, were none too happy at having to supply water gratis to the canal and then see the FR sell it on to the ironworks. The Act removed the obligation on the Local Board whilst giving it a half share of any income from the sale of water to the NLI&SCo.

It was to be the end of May 1883 before the Furness Engineer approached the Board of Trade to inspect the branch for passenger traffic. The inspector, Major General Hutchinson RE, visited Ulverston on 23 June. In his report he remarked, in passing, that part of the branch had been in use for mineral trains prior to his inspection. He was generally in favour of the construction but was dissatisfied with the strength of the under-bridges. These consisted of four cast-iron girders between the parapets, holding the bridge deck and rails between them, one track between a pair of girders. At the inspector's insistence, additional girders were placed between each existing pair during July 1883. Although all were subsequently rebuilt, one incomplete but original example remains: that in the field beyond Priory station. One bridge – over the canal – was notable for its novelty, being just above water level and arranged such that the main deck could be withdrawn to allow a 26 foot opening for shipping.

Signal boxes were erected at three points. Ulverston Canal box was situated where the old Canal branch was diverted from running into the ironworks sidings into a junction with the Bardsea branch (the sidings in the ironworks being largely truncated at this northern end rather than linking them into the new branch). Canal box also controlled the sliding canal bridge and a level crossing over the tow path on the eastern bank. The next box was at North Lonsdale Crossing, an impressive structure with buttressed walls and some windows having wooden shutters in place of glazing. The design matched contemporaries built at Ramsden Dock Station, Park South and Park North. As well as protecting the level crossing over the road to Canal Foot, North Lonsdale Crossing controlled the main access from the branch into the ironworks, together with a siding onto Gradwell's tramway to allow access to Sadler's and other works. The tramway was also diverted to run under the branch, thus allowing limestone to be taken into the ironworks without having to cross the branch on the level. The final signal box was at Priory and was built into the station building. This controlled the siding and run-around at the station, with the home and starting signals protecting Priory crossing. Up on the Canal branch a small signal box or shunting frame was provided to control Canal Sidings adjacent to the paper mill.

Passenger services between Ulverston and Priory, with reversal at Plumpton Junction, commenced with the timetable of 27 June 1883. Because of the delay in doing this, the Furness Railway Company was obliged to compensate the Conishead Priory Hydropathic Co. to the tune of £500! The service for the next 33 years was to be never more than two trains in each direction; after two or three years only a single return trip was scheduled. The service relied on first-class passengers and other guests bound for the Hydro: the journey was so roundabout and the direct road from Ulverston to Bardsea was a short and easy route. An intermediate platform was opened at North Lonsdale Crossing in June 1888.

At some point after the opening of the Bardsea branch one further industry was set up, possibly a subsidiary of the NLI&SCo., the Ulverston Wireworks. This was located south of Sadler's chemical works and close to Gradwell's brickworks. It was served by an extension into the siding serving Sadler's works. Meanwhile Gradwell and Strongitharm's grand plan for villas between the new railway and the Bardsea road came to naught. The fields remain as arable land to this day.

Limestone continued to be ferried across the fields from Gascow Quarry to the North Lonsdale Ironworks for around thirty years. An internal narrow-gauge railway was used within the quarry. Initially it seems Gradwell's own locomotive was used but, for most of the time, the NLI&SCo. worked the trains. In June 1897 the NLI&SCo. had gained a mineral lease on land at Plumpton Hall, behind Plumpton Junction, and in the coming years opened up a new limestone quarry which came into full production following a further lease in February 1908. Gradwell's were given notice of the NLI&SCo.'s intention in 1903 and the two parties spent some time in dispute before Gascow Quarry

was abandoned. The tramway was taken up in 1911. At some time the NLI&SCo. gained permission from the Furness Railway Company to operate the trains of limestone from Plumpton Quarry to the Ironworks with their own locomotives. This agreement could have been a result of the NLI&SCo. considering the erection of an aerial ropeway between the two points in 1910, thus bypassing the Bardsea branch. The NLI&SCo. limestone trains continued to shuttle up and down the northern section of the Bardsea branch at varying frequencies, depending on demand, until the blast furnaces were finally closed in 1938.

Iron ore for the ironworks came from several sources. Initially the supply came from Harrison Ainslie's mines at Lindal and Kennedy Brothers' mines at Roanhead, the trains therefore running from Park and Lindal Ore Depots. Before 1881, these would have run to Plumpton Junction, the locomotive run around its train and proceeded back towards Ulverston in order to back down onto the Canal branch. With the availability of the Bardsea branch, the routing was easier, even with reversal at Plumpton Junction. In 1914 Harrison Ainslie ceased trading and the NLI&SCo. bought their Whitriggs Mines. Sources widened in 1918 when NLI&SCo. became part-owners of the Ullcoats Mines in West Cumberland. The Great Depression brought many British businesses to their knees. The ironworks were going through a rough period, leading to the furnaces being blown out in October 1931. Whitriggs Mines were closed and in November the NLI&SCo. was taken over by the Millom & Askam Iron & Steel Co. For a while production at North Lonsdale was halted, but it resumed briefly from April 1937 until one of the two furnaces in blast collapsed on 15 August 1938, when iron making at Ulverston ceased. By this time the Millom parent company was importing iron ore from their mines at Aquife in Spain (civil war permitting) through Barrow Docks.

Coke was sourced primarily from County Durham throughout the working life of the blast furnaces at North Lonsdale. These were routed over the North Eastern Railway via Barnard Castle, Kirkby Stephen and Tebay from where the LNWR took them south to Carnforth. In the early days, the wagonloads of coke (and presumably tar for Sadler's) were shunted at Plumpton Junction from trains headed to Lindal and points south and west before being shunted up to Canal Viaduct and down onto the Canal branch. With the opening of the Bardsea branch to mineral trains, dedicated coke trains could run through from Carnforth. After 1916 wartime stringencies led to the FR and LNWR agreeing to routeing the coke for North Lonsdale directly from Tebay via Sandside. From that date locomotives from both companies were used. Coke traffic

Bardsea Branch. *An ex-MR 2F 0-6-0 and its train of fuel oil leaves Plumpton Junction for Glaxo circa 1953. The branch had been singled with the old down line, nearest the camera, reduced to a siding in 1952.*
(CRA Photo Library ref. JA1120)

was sporadic during the 1930s with the ironworks closed and briefly resumed during 1937-8. Sadler's tar traffic had ceased between 1926 and 1928 with the closure of the chemical works at Sand Hall. The works was dismantled in 1931 but the siding wasn't removed until March 1936.

In addition to the mineral trains to North Lonsdale Ironworks, daily trip workings served the various sidings: at Priory (where there was a gasworks for Conishead Priory), Sadler's chemical works (tar and coal in, pitch and chemicals out), the Ulverston Brick Works (coal in and bricks out), the Wire Works (coal in and wire out), North Lonsdale Ironworks (coal in, as well as coke, with pig iron and foundry products, including ingot moulds, out), Furness Paper Mills (coal and possibly china clay in, paper goods out), Messrs Randall & Porter's warehouse alongside the New Basin (hides in and leather out), Ulverston Gasworks (coal in and possibly tar out) and Messrs Charnley's timber yard, on the site of the erstwhile Canal Head Foundry (coal and timber in). It should be noted that the Ulverston Gasworks hadn't received its siding alongside the canal until the first half of 1902.

During the first half of the 20th century, advantage was taken of the slag available in substantial quantities for little or no charge, at the ironworks. From December 1909 to the end of 1922, slag was extracted for use as railway ballast by C W Hunter on his FR ballast contracts. A narrow gauge railway was used to carry slag to the crusher, from where it was loaded into main line ballast wagons. Hunter lost this contract at grouping. The 1920s saw a significant growth in the use of motor transport for which the existing roads were not totally suitable. New roads were planned by County authorities across the country and old roads rebuilt and widened to meet new regulations. In North Lancashire and south Westmorland, two notable roads built at the time were the Ulverston – Barrow coast road, built jointly by the Ulverston Rural District Council, Ulverston Urban District Council and Barrow County Borough between 1920 and 1924, and the Heversham bypass (Prince's Way) opened in 1927. The slag banks were let to the Irlam Tar Macadam Co. from November 1924, who set up a slag crusher and associated narrow gauge railways and produced tarmacadam under the title of North Lonsdale Tarmacadam Co. This company continued in production until around 1936, by which time it was a subsidiary of Thomas W Ward. The plant was dismantled in 1940.

Passenger traffic was sparse, and one must question the FR's logic for providing the service to North Lonsdale Crossing and Priory for as long as it did. In 1896 the villagers of Bardsea petitioned the Furness to extend the Bardsea branch to Red Lane (it must still have owned the land). Although plans were prepared for a new passenger station,

no further action was taken and the scheme dropped. It took the privations and economies of the Great War to halt the service, it ceasing from 6 March 1916. By that time it was unusual for the train to carry a passenger! The track remained in situ at Priory many more years. The Hydro remained in business into the 1920s. In 1928 Conishead Priory was acquired by the Durham Miners Welfare Committee as a convalescent home, similar to the several earlier establishments at Grange. Eligible miners were allowed to stay at the Priory for two weeks, coming from the North-East on special fortnightly trains run to Ulverston for many years. The LMS resisted the option to run the trains to Priory despite the track remaining in place. From 1940 to 1945 the Priory was commandeered to become the largest Military Hospital in the North-West. In 1941 the Engineers Department at Barrow produced plans to remove the track beyond Priory Crossing. However this didn't occur for another 12 years. Although feasible, the LMS never ran an ambulance train down the branch: the numbers of wounded travelling to the hospital at any one time never justified this.

Some investment was made on the branch in 1931 when Ulverston Canal signal box was replaced by a standard LMS structure, located alongside the Bardsea branch (its predecessor facing the canal). The box opened from 7 December 1931. Ironically the North Lonsdale Ironworks had ceased production two months earlier. Rationalisation took place two years later when in March 1933 the section between Canal and North Lonsdale Crossing became Up and Down sidings. North Lonsdale Crossing closed as a block post. Things looked up in November 1937 when the ironworks resumed production and North Lonsdale box was probably reopened. The good times didn't last long, however: pig iron production only lasted until August the following year. As a result, in August 1938 the branch beyond Canal officially became worked as sidings and North Lonsdale Crossing closed, except to work the crossing gates.

The redundant blast furnaces remained in situ until demolition in 1947, whilst foundry work continued at North Lonsdale Ironworks until the end of 1949. In September 1945, part of the site was sold to Glaxo Laboratories Ltd., who built their pharmaceutical plant, opened in 1948. This was served by rail and, for a short period during 1948-9, shunted by NLI&SCo. locomotives until their own Andrew Barclay fireless loco arrived. It would be 1955 before the redundant ironworks buildings had been cleared and Glaxo extended their plant across the site. The main structures from the ironworks retained by Glaxo were the boiler house and chimney.

Ulverston. *An ex-MR 2F 0-6-0 shunts the sidings at Glaxo circa 1953. Ulverston Canal signalbox formerly stood adjacent to the distant wagons, where the Canal branch leaves the rump of the Bardsea branch. (CRA Photo Library ref. JA1118)*

The siding into Charnley's timber yard had been cut back by 1932, leaving the Gasworks siding as the northernmost siding on the Canal branch. The Furness Paper Mills closed in the 1930s. The site was taken over, during the Second World War, by Messrs Armstrong Siddeley for the repair of aircraft engines. At the end of the war, the site was taken over by Messrs Wade, who later operated the site as Powdered Metal Products Ltd., producing shell casings and metal framed furniture. The site remained rail served until Powdered Metal Products ceased production on the site in 1955. This left Ulverston Gasworks as the only customer on the Canal branch. This continued to receive coal by rail until the branch closed in late1966. The canal itself was officially closed in 1946, having been little used for nearly thirty years.

Significant rationalization of the Bardsea branch took place in 1952-3. In that October buffer-stops were put across the track at the north side of Priory crossing and the track beyond was taken up. The remaining track between there and North Lonsdale Crossing was given over, like many redundant branch lines, to wagon storage. At the same time Plumpton Junction was simplified and the Bardsea branch reduced to a single-line siding to serve Glaxo and the Canal branch. Canal signal box was closed, the upper part and locking frame being reused at Cark. The canal bridge was fixed across the canal and associated (and long disused) hydraulic plant scrapped.

In 1964, following the impact of the Beeching report and the rationalization of goods facilities across the former Furness Railway, negotiations were opened between BR and Glaxo. These culminated in 1966 with Glaxo purchasing all the remaining railway plant on the Bardsea branch from and including the canal bridge. The Canal branch was closed and track removed at the same time. After that date BR locomotives would propel trains down the branch from Plumpton Junction. Glaxo used their fireless steam locomotive to pull the wagons over the canal bridge and into the plant. It was to remain in use until retirement in May 1989. Traffic to Glaxo was largely in the form of oil for its boilers.

From May 1989 until 27 April1994, when Glaxochem (as it had become) received its last shipment of oil by rail, the branch was operated by Glaxo's own ex-BR diesel shunter. Not being fireproofed, it was not allowed to enter the pharmaceutical plant. It was thus limited to propelling wagons from Plumpton Junction and across the canal bridge and through the gates of the plant. The branch then went into its final decay.

Ironically the final train to use the branch was a passenger train, and, in the tradition of passenger services on the branch, that train carried only a few passengers. On the night of 22 May 1995 the Royal Train was stabled on the branch. Track remained in place until the closure of Plumpton Junction signal box on 19 March 2000. The branch was lifted in the following May, leaving the track bed from Plumpton to the Canal towpath and bridge as an unofficial, and overgrown, footpath.

(2 30 for Private Use.)

On Christmas Day the Trains marked CH. only will run.

FURNESS AND ULVERSTONE AND LANCASTER RAILWAYS.

WORKING TIME TABLE FOR DECEMBER, 1860.

PASSENGER TRAINS

UP.	Week Days 1 (CH.) 1,2,3	2 1 & 2	3 (CH) 1,2,3	4 (CH.) 1,2,3	Sundays 1 1,2,3	2 1,2,3	3 1,2,3
	a.m.	p.m.	p.m.	p.m.	a.m.	a.m	p.m.
Coniston L'k dep	8 15	12 5	.. ..	6 45	.. ..	8 15	6 10
Torver	8 22	A	.. ..	6 52	.. ..	8 25	6 20
Woodland	8 30	.. ..	.. ..	7 0	.. ..	8 35	6 30
Broughton	8 40	12 30	.. ..	7 10	.. ..	8 45	6 40
Foxfield Junc.	8 50	12†40	.. ..	7 20	.. ..	8 55	6 50
Kirkby	8 55	A	.. ..	7 25	.. ..	9 0	6 55
Barrow	8 50	12 50	3 10	7 30	7 20	.. ..	20
Furness Abbey	9 0	1 5	3 20	7 45	7 30	9 15	7 15
Dalton	9 15	1 10	3 25	7 50	7 35	9 20	7 20
Lindal	9 20	.. ..	3 30	7 55	7 40	9 25	7 25
Ulverstone	9 35	1 25	3 40	8 10	7 50	9 35	7†40
Leven Viaduct	.. ..	.. ..	.. ..	8†15	.. ..	.. ..	.. ..
Cark & Cartmel	9 50	1†40	3†55	8 30	8 6	.. ..	8 0
Kents Bank	A	.. ..	4 3	A	8 4	.. ..	8 8
Grange	10† 5	1 50	4†10	8 45	8 23	.. ..	8 16
Arnside	10 13	.. ..	4 18	A	8 3[illegible]	.. ..	8 25
Silverdale	10 20	.. ..	4 25	9 15	8 38	.. ..	8 33
Carnforth ar	10 30	2 15	4 4[illegible]	9 3[illegible]	8 50	.. ..	8 45

DOWN.	Week Days 1 (CH.) 1,2,3	2 (CH.) 1,2,3	3 (CH.) 1 & 2	4 (CH.) 1,2,3	Sundays 1 1,2,3	2 1,2,3	3 1,2,3	4 1,2,3
	a.m.	a.m.	p.m.	p.m	a.m.	a.m.	p.m.	p.m.
Carnforth.. dep.	.. ..	10 50	3 45	6 45	.. ..	9 0	.. ..	6 40
Silverdale	.. ..	11 0	3†55	6 55	.. ..	9 10	.. ..	6 59
Arnside	.. ..	11 8	.. ..	A	.. ..	9 18	.. ..	6 57
Grange	.. ..	11†16	4†10	7 10	.. ..	9 26	.. ..	7 5
Kents Bank	.. ..	11 24	.. ..	A	.. ..	9 34	.. ..	7 12
Cark & Cartmel	.. ..	11 32	4 20	7†20	.. ..	9 42	.. ..	7 20
Leven Viaduct	.. ..	.. ..	.. ..	.. ..	.. ..	.. ..	.. ..	.. ..
Ulverstone	6 30	11 50	4†35	7 40	8 10	10 0	6 0	7†10
Lindal	6 40	12 0	4 45	7 50	8 20	10 10	6 10	7 50
Dalton	6 45	12 5	4 50	7 55	8 25	10 15	6 15	7 55
Barrow	5 50	12 10	4 50	.. ..	7 20	.. ..	5 20	.. ..
Furness Abbey	6 55	12 15	5 5	8 0	8 30	10 20	6 25	8 0
Kirkby	7 10	12 30	5†20	.. ..	8 45	—	6 40	—
Foxfield Junc.	7 20	12†40	5 25	.. ..	8 55	.. ..	6 50	.. ..
Broughton	7 30	12 50	5 35	.. ..	9 0	.. ..	6 55	.. ..
Woodland	7 40	1 0	A	.. ..	9 10	.. ..	7 5	.. ..
Torver	7 50	1 10	5 50	.. ..	9 20	.. ..	7 15	.. ..
Coniston Lake	8 0	1 20	6 0	.. ..	9 30	.. ..	7 25	.. ..

A Stops by Signal if required.

BARROW AND CONISTON BRANCHES.

UP.	Week Days 1 1,2,3 Mixd	2 1,2,3 class	3 1,2,3 class	4 1 & 2 Exp.	5 1,2,3 class	6 1 & 2 class	7 1,2,3 class	8 1,2,3 class	Sundays 1 1,2,3 class	2 1,2,3 class	3 1,2,3 class	4 1,2,3 class
	a.m.	a.m.	a.m.	p.m.	p.m.	p.m.	p.m.	p.m.	a.m.	a.m.	p.m.	p.m.
F'wood ..leave Piel Pier about	CH.	CH.	CH.		CH.	CH.		CH.				
Barrow ..leave	5 50	8 50	12 0	12 50	3 10	4 50	5 30	7 30	7 20	.. ..	5 20	.. ..
Furness Abbey	A	9 0	12 15	1 5	3 20	5 5	5 40	7 45	7 30	9 15	5 30	7 15
Dalton	A	9 15	.. ..	1 10	3 25	.. ..	5 45	7 50	7 35	9 20	5 35	7 20
Lindal	A	9 20	.. ..	.. ..	3 30	.. ..	5 50	7 55	7 40	9 25	5 40	7 25
Ulverston ..ar.	6 20	9 30	.. ..	1 25	3 40	.. ..	6 0	8 5	7 50	9 35	5 50	7 35
Kirkby	7 10	.. ..	12 30	.. ..	.. ..	5†20	.. ..	.. ..	8 45	.. ..	6 40	.. ..
Foxfield	7 20	.. ..	12†40	.. ..	.. ..	5 25	.. ..	.. ..	8 55	.. ..	6 50	.. ..
Broughton	7 30	.. ..	12 50	.. ..	.. ..	5 35	.. ..	.. ..	9 0	.. ..	6 55	.. ..
Woodland	7 40	.. ..	1 0	.. ..	.. ..	A	.. ..	.. ..	9 10	.. ..	7 5	.. ..
Torver	7 50	.. ..	1 10	.. ..	.. ..	5 50	.. ..	.. ..	9 20	.. ..	7 15	.. ..
Coniston L'k	8 0	.. ..	1 20	.. ..	.. ..	6 0	.. ..	.. ..	9 30	.. ..	7 25	.. ..

DOWN.	Week Days 1 (CH.) 1,2,3 class	2 (CH.) 1,2,3 class	3 1 & 2 class	4 (CH.) 1 & 2 Exp.	5 (CH.) 1,2,3 class	6 (CH.) 1,2,3 class	Sundays 1 1,2,3 class	2 1,2,3 class	3 1,2,3 class	4 1,2,3 class
	a.m.	a.m.	p.m.	p.m.	p.m.	p.m.	a.m.	a.m.	p.m.	p.m.
Coniston L'k	8 15	.. ..	12 5	.. ..	6 45	.. ..	.. ..	8 15	.. ..	6 10
Torver	8 22	.. ..	A	.. ..	6 52	.. ..	.. ..	8 25	.. ..	6 20
Woodland	8 30	.. ..	.. ..	.. ..	7 0	.. ..	.. ..	8 35	.. ..	6 30
Broughton	8 40	.. ..	12 30	.. ..	7 10	.. ..	.. ..	8 45	.. ..	6 40
Foxfield	8 50	.. ..	12†40	.. ..	7 20	.. ..	.. ..	8 55	.. ..	6 50
Kirkby	8 55	.. ..	A	.. ..	7 25	.. ..	.. ..	9 0	.. ..	6 55
Ulverston, dep	9 0	11 50	.. ..	4 35	.. ..	7 40	8 10	10 0	6 0	7 40
Lindal	9 10	12 0	.. ..	4 45	.. ..	7 50	8 20	10 10	6 10	7 50
Dalton	9 20	12 5	.. ..	4 50	.. ..	7 55	8 25	10 15	6 15	7 55
Furness Abbey	9 25	12 15	1 5	5 0	7 45	8 0	8 30	10 20	6 25	8 0
Barrow, arrive	9 35	12 25	1 15	5 10	7 55	8 10	.. ..	10 30	.. ..	8 10
Piel Pier										
Dep. f'r F'wood										

A Stops by Signal if required.

ULVERSTON MARKET DAYS. { On Thursdays a Train will leave Carnforth for Ulverstone at 7 40, Grange 8 40, and Cark 9 10 a.m.
THIRD CLASS Return Tickets will be issued from all Stations to Ulverstone for No. 1 Up Train—Returning by any train Down to Barrow, Broughton and Coniston.

ROOSE.—Nos. 2, 3, 5, and 7 Up, and 1, 4, and 6 Down Trains, on Week Days and Sunday Trains, will stop when required.

On Christmas Day the Trains marked CH. only will run.

GOODS TRAINS FOR DECEMBER, 1860.

UP.	1 CH. Goods Local & L. and Y. Ore arrive	dep.	2 CH. Whitehaven Ore. arrive	dep.	3 CH. Staffordshire Ore. arrive	dep.	4 CH. Local Goods and Slate. arrive	dep.	5 CH. Slate and Ore arrive	dep.	6 CH. Through Goods arrive	dep.	7 CH. Ore and Pass. from U'stn. arrive	dep.
Whitehaven			.. ..	.. ..			.. ..	.. ..			.. ..	1 5		
Coniston			.. ..	.. ..			.. ..	12 5			.. ..	.. ..		
Broughton			.. ..	.. ..			.. ..	1 0			.. ..	4 30		
Foxfield Jun.			.. ..	7 50			1 5	1 10			4 35	4 55		
Kirkby			.. ..	.. ..			1 15	1 30			5 5	5† 21		
Dunnerholme			.. ..	.. ..			1 40	1 45			.. ..	.. ..		
Parks			8 10	8 20	1 5	1 15	1 55	2 10	2 35	2 45	5 40	5 50		
Furness Abbey			.. ..	.. ..	.. ..	.. ..	2 20	2 25	.. ..	.. ..	.. ..	.. ..		
Barrow	.. ..	5 40	.. ..	7 0	.. ..	12 4[illegible]	2 40		.. ..	2 10	.. ..	.. ..	.. ..	5 30
Dalton	5 55	6 0	8 30	8 3[illegible]	1 25	1 30			2 55	3 0	6 0	6 10	5 43	5 4[illegible]
Crooklands	.. ..	.. ..	8 40	8 50	1 35	1 40			3 5	3 10	.. ..	.. ..	.. ..	.. ..
Lindal	-6-5	-6-20	-8-55	-9-4[illegible]	-1-45	-2-30			-3-15	-4-10	-6-20	-6-25	-5-48	-7-15
Ulverstone	6 35	6 50	10 0	10 20	2 45	2 50			4 25	4† 35	6 4[illegible]	7† 1	7 30	8 10
Leven Viaduct	.. ..	.. ..	.. ..	.. ..	.. ..	.. ..			.. ..	.. ..	.. ..	.. ..	.. ..	8† 5
Cark	7 5	7 10	10† 40	10 50	.. ..	.. ..			4 55	5 5	7† 2[illegible]	7 25	8 25	8 30
Kents Bank	7 15	7 20	10 55	11 0	.. ..	.. ..			.. ..	.. ..	.. ..	.. ..	.. ..	.. ..
Grange	7 25	7 30	11 10	11† 20	3 20	3† 22			5 20	5 30	7† 40	7 50	8 40	8 45
Meathop	7 35	7 45	11 30	11 40	3 30	3 3[illegible]			.. ..	.. ..	.. ..	.. ..	.. ..	.. ..
Arnside	7 50	7 55	11 50	11 55	.. ..	.. ..			.. ..	.. ..	.. ..	.. ..	.. ..	.. ..
Silverdale	8 †0	8 5	12 5	12 10	3 50	3† 56			5† 15	5 50	8 10	8 15	9 10	9 15
Carnforth	8 15	.. ..	12 20	.. ..	4 10	.. ..			6 0	.. ..	8 2[illegible]	.. ..	9 3[illegible]	.. ..
	†Down Goods. at Silverdale.		†down goods at Cark. † Dwn. pass. at Grage.		†Down Goods at Grange. † Down Exp at Silverdale.				†Dn gds & Exp. at Uston. † Down gds Silverdale.		†Dn. Exp. Kby. †Dn g'ds U'stn †Dn pass Cark. †Dn gds. at Gr.		†Down goods at Leven Viaduct.	

DOWN.	1 CH. Tranships from U'ston to W'haven and Con., and Pass. arrive	dep.	2 CH. Goods and Ore Waggons. arrive	dep.	3 CH. Ore Waggons & Local Goods. arrive	dep.	4 CH. Thro' & rdsd. gds. & Lancaster tranships. arrive	dep.	5 CH. Local Goods & empty Ore waggons. arriv	dep.	6 CH. Staff. Empties & Local Goods. arrive	dep.	7 CH. Ore Waggons and Thro' Goods arrive	dep.
Carnforth			.. ..	7 4[illegible]	.. ..	9 25	.. ..	12 30	.. ..	2 40	.. ..	5 30	.. ..	6 50
Silverdale			7 55	8† 0	9 3[illegible]	9 40	.. ..	.. ..	.. ..	.. ..	5 40	5† 46	7 [illegible]0	7 5
Arnside			8 10	8 15	.. ..	.. ..	.. ..	.. ..	.. ..	.. ..	5 55	6 [illegible]0	.. ..	.. ..
Meathop			8 20	8 25	.. ..	.. ..	12 50	1 0	3 0	3 10	.. ..	.. ..	.. ..	.. ..
Grange			8 35	8 4[illegible]	10† 0	10 6	1 10	1 20	3† 20	3 30	6 10	6 15	7 30	7† 41
Kents Bank			.. ..	.. ..	10 15	10 20	.. ..	.. ..	.. ..	.. ..	6 20	6 25	.. ..	.. ..
Cark			8 55	9 10	10 30	10† 41	1† 35	1 45	3 45	3† 56	6 35	6 40	7 55	8 0
Leven Viaduct			.. ..	.. ..	10 55	11 0	.. ..	.. ..	4 10	4 15	.. ..	.. ..	.. ..	8† 15
Ulverstone	.. ..	6 30	9 3[illegible]	10 30	11 10	11 30	2 5	2 25	4† 25	4 40	7† 0	7 15	8 20	8 30
Lindal	-6-38	-6-40	-10-45	-10-55	-11† 45	-12-5	-2-40	-2-45	-4-55	-5-0	-7-30	-7-40	-8-45	-8-50
Crooklands	.. ..	.. ..	11 0	11 5	12 10	12 15	.. ..	.. ..	5 5	5 10	.. ..	.. ..	8 55	9 0
Dalton	6 43	6 45	11 10	11 15	12 20	12 25	2 50	3 0	5 15	5 20	7 45	7 50	9 5	9 10
Furness Abbey	6 50	6 55	.. ..	.. ..	.. ..	.. ..	.. ..	.. ..	5 55	6 0	.. ..	.. ..	.. ..	.. ..
Barrow	.. ..	.. ..	.. ..	8 0	1 0	.. ..	.. ..	2 10	6 15	.. ..	8 5	.. ..	9 25	.. ..
Parks	.. ..	.. ..	11 25	11 35	12 35	12 45	3 10	3 20	5 30	5 45				
Dunnerholme	.. ..	.. ..	11 45	11 50			.. ..	.. ..	.. ..	.. ..				
Kirkby	7 8	7 10	12 0	12 5			3 35	3 4[illegible]	.. ..	.. ..				
Foxfield Jun.	7 15	7 20	12 10	12 20			3 50	4 0	.. ..	.. ..				
Broughton	7 25	7 3[illegible]	12 25	12 5[illegible]			4 5	5 3[illegible]	.. ..	.. ..				
Coniston	8 0	.. ..	1 20	.. ..			6 0	.. ..	.. ..	.. ..				
Whitehaven	12 45													
			† Up Goods at Silverdale. On Thdays this train brings mks pass		†.Up Pass. at Grge. † Up gds ark. † Sht Lindal down pass.		† Up Express at Cark.		† Up Ore Grge †Up pass Cark. † Up g'ds & wt dn Exp U'stn		†Up Ore at S'dale †Up Gds at U'stn.		† Up Gds at Gr. † Up mixed at Leven Viaduct.	

When not required from Foxfield will leave Barrow at 7 50 a.m.

On Christmas Day No 6 from Broughton will run No. 7 from Ulverston, and a Special Engine will leave Coniston at 11 a.m. for Carnforth, crossing No. 2 down pass. at Park, and No. 4 down goods at Cark.

BARROW ORE TRAINS,

FOR DECEMBER, 1860.

Lindal Trains.

Barrow ..leave	7 15	9 30	11 40	1 35	3 30	6 15
Lindal ...arrive	7 55	10 5	12 15	2 15	4 10	6 50
Lindal....leave	8 10	10 15	12 25	2 30	5 25	7 0
Barrow.. arrive	8 50	10 55	1 5	3 10	6 0	7 40

Park Trains.

Barrow...leave	*7 0	8 0	10 40	12 40	.. ..	2 10	3 15	.. ..
Park ....arrive	7 20	8 20	11 5	1 5	.. ..	2 35	3 40	.. ..
Park......leave	.. ..	9 30	11 15	12 45	2 10	.. ..	4 5	5 45
Barrow ..arrive	.. ..	10 0	11 40	1 0	2 40	.. ..	4 30	6 15

Goods Trains which have to shunt for Passenger Trains must arrive at the Crossing Place as much as possible before the time of the Passenger Train.

Trains are to cross each other at the places marked thus † and should anything occur to prevent the arrival of either Train at the appointed crossing place, the other Train must not proceed until it has been clearly arranged by Telegraph or other means where the crossing is to take place.

The Ore Trains must arrive at and depart from Stations as near as possible to times fixed. Every exertion must be made to keep clear of Through Trains.

G. M. O., Novr., 1860 (By Order) JAMES RAMSDEN, S. & G. M.

FR Working Timetable for December 1860. *The Furness worked trains over the U&LR as if it were part of its own system. The notes on the timetable show just how much the safety of the railway was in the hands of the train crews.*

(CRA Walker Collection)

Train Services

9

Meathop. *The 10-50 am Workington to London Euston train (W254) passes Meathop heading for Arnside on 25 June 1958. Ex-LMS Class 5MT No. 45386 pilots ex-LMS 6P 'Patriot' No. 45546* Fleetwood. *This train was piloted between Barrow (where additional carriages were added) and Carnforth, usually by a locomotive from Crewe North shed. On this day such plans have gone awry as the pilot locomotive was one of Barrow's allocation.* (CRA Photo Library ref. PEK391)

FIRST, SOME BACKGROUND on FR train services generally. When the line first opened, Furness Railway passenger trains effectively ran on a main line from Carnforth to Barrow, with a branch to Broughton – from 1859 to Coniston. For the first 11 months of the U&LR's existence, passengers for Whitehaven would change from FR to W&FJR trains at Broughton, but from the August 1858 timetable passengers would change at the new junction at Foxfield. Concurrently the 'Millwood' curve, opened at the same time, allowed some Broughton (and later Coniston) trains to avoid reversal at Furness Abbey. From 1866, when the W&FJR became part of the FR empire, Barrow and Coniston each found itself at the end of a branch line, with the FR main line now running from Carnforth to Whitehaven. A year later saw the opening of the Carnforth – Wennington line, jointly owned by the FR and Midland Railway. This allowed the introduction of express trains from London, St Pancras and Leeds to the pier at Piel in connection with steamers to Douglas and Belfast. 1869 saw the opening of the branch line to Lakeside with trains from Ulverston (and occasional excursions from beyond Carnforth) to Lakeside, with connecting steam yachts on Windermere. The other major event affecting the U&LR line at this period was the opening of the 'Kendal' branch from Arnside to Hincaster Junction, south of Oxenholme on the LNWR in 1876. This allowed a passenger service from Grange or Arnside to Kendal.

It was not until 1882 that Barrow found itself back on the main line, when the Barrow and Park Loop lines eventually opened, allowing trains to run from Barrow to Askam direct instead of via Furness Abbey. A year earlier boat trains had been moved from Piel Pier to the new Ramsden Dock station in Barrow. 1882 also saw the commencement of a basic train service on the Bardsea branch, with its train from Ulverston reversing at Plumpton Junction. Apart from the closure of the various branch lines this situation essentially holds today.

At first few passenger trains passed along the U&LR. Although the U&LR had made arrangements for through running to Lancaster, it is hard to tell from the timetables if this actually occurred. The December 1860 working timetable shows that stations were not favoured to be served by every passenger train. Of the three westbound trains from Carnforth to Barrow, only the 9-00 am service stopped at all stations on the U&LR. The 3-45 pm express carried first and second class passengers only, and stopped at Silverdale, Grange and Cark before Ulverston, whilst the 6-45 pm train stopped at Arnside and Kents Bank as required. The Thursdays only (Ulverston Market Day) carriages were tagged onto the 7-40 am Carnforth to Coniston goods and empty ore wagons train as far as Ulverston. It served only Grange and Cark. Eastbound there were four passenger trains. The 8-15 am from Coniston to Carnforth stopped at Kents Bank as required, while the 12-50 pm express (first and second class passengers only) omitted Kents Bank, Arnside and Silverdale. The 5-30 pm from Barrow stopped at all stations, while the 7-30 pm from Barrow, omitting Silverdale and calling at Kents Bank if required, also carried ore from Ulverston to Carnforth.

An exception on the eastbound services was when John Brogden instructed the driver of a train to proceed on to Lancaster, much to the annoyance of the Lancaster and Carlisle Railway. Connections could be made from westbound trains at Furness Abbey for onward journeys to Coniston or Whitehaven. Sundays saw two trains in each direction. Coaches were available at Cark to take passengers to Newby Bridge for the Windermere steamers.

By the 1870s things had improved somewhat; an 1877 timetable shows eight passenger trains in each direction. Of the westbound trains, four were to Whitehaven (with connections at Dalton for Barrow), three were to Barrow only, whilst one, the Belfast Boat Train from St Pancras, ran to Piel Pier and Barrow. The morning Whitehaven mail train,

The train for Kendal via Sandside *stands in the Up platform at Grange whilst the locomotive of a Barrow-bound train lets off steam in this photograph taken probably in the later 1880s. The locomotive on the 'Kendal Tommy', FR Sharp, Stewart 2-2-2WT No. 37 of 1866, stands at the head of a train made up of a horse box, leading, and brown carriages. Locomotives of this type were the mainstay of passenger trains on the Ulverston & Lancaster line from opening until the early 1870s when they were superseded by Sharp, Stewart 2-4-0 tender locomotives, one of which is possibly hauling the Down train. The well tanks continued to haul branch line trains until the early 1890s when they were again displaced. The 2-4-0s were used on the main line passenger traffic until 1890 when the first 4-4-0s arrived on the Furness and helped share the traffic. Further 4-4-0s appeared in 1896, taking over much of the main line work from the 2-4-0s. Seven of them were rebuilt in 1891-96 as 2-4-2 tank locomotives for use on the increasingly heavier branch-line trains.*
(Photographer Gilbert Wilson of Grange, Authors collection)

Meathop. *On 25 June 1958 ex-LMS 4MT 2-6-4T No. 42317 and the 1-20 pm Carnforth to Barrow train approach Meathop sidings from Arnside.*
(CRA Photo Library ref. PEK390)

Kents Bank. Ex-LMS Class 5MT 4-6-0 No. 44927 pulls the 8-50 am Blackpool-Coniston train out of Kents Bank station on 10 July 1956. (CRA Photo Library ref. PEJ481)

the midday Carnforth – Barrow and the Belfast Boat train for Piel stopped only at Grange and Ulverston on the U&LR section. Eastbound trains largely terminated at Carnforth, with three connecting at Carnforth F&M Junction for Midland Railway trains towards Leeds and Bradford. The morning Boat Train to St Pancras did not stop beyond Furness Abbey. Sundays saw a sparse service of three trains each way (one in each direction to Whitehaven with the others to and from Barrow). Again the Carnforth – Whitehaven Mail train stopped only at Grange and Ulverston on the U&LR section. The Kendal branch trains, nicknamed 'Kendal Tommy' after a long-serving member of the regular crew, ran to and from Grange at this time, three trains a day making the journey to and from Kendal. At the west end of the U&LR section, the Lakeside branch was served by five passenger trains to and from Ulverston on weekdays with three trips each way on Sundays.

By the 1880s the services along the Furness main line reached what was to be effectively the standard for the rest of FR days. With minor variations, there would be around 11 eastbound trains and between 10 and 13 westbound. Of these, five or six would be running through to or from Whitehaven. Three Down and four Up 'expresses' called only at Grange, whilst the morning Down Belfast Boat train ran non-stop, except on Mondays when a call was made at

Grange. In this period the Kendal branch saw about five return trips, except Sundays. Only three or four would run beyond Arnside to Grange. The Lakeside branch was still served by five return trips from Ulverston, with three each way on Sundays. There were, of course exceptions, such as the through FR trains from Grange to Morecambe in the summer season and Thursdays only trains to Ulverston.

Between the summer of 1887 and December 1916 the Furness Railway operated Slip Carriages, often only during the summer, and many using Midland Railway vehicles running through from Leeds or London. Grange was to see them throughout the period. The slip carriage would be frowned upon in these safety-conscious days, but then it was seen as quite acceptable to allow a carriage full of people to be uncoupled from a moving train. With the guard's careful application of the brake, the carriage would glide gently to a stop in the station platform. It would then be shunted into a siding before being returned to its starting point by another train.

No particular trend can be followed over the first five years of slip workings. At first, four trains 'slipped' at Grange: in the afternoon from a Whitehaven – Carnforth train and from the Douglas boat train (from Leeds), and in the evening again from a Whitehaven – Carnforth train and from a Carnforth – Barrow train. In fact, such was

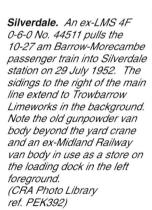

Silverdale. An ex-LMS 4F 0-6-0 No. 44511 pulls the 10-27 am Barrow-Morecambe passenger train into Silverdale station on 29 July 1952. The sidings to the right of the main line extend to Trowbarrow Limeworks in the background. Note the old gunpowder van body beyond the yard crane and an ex-Midland Railway van body in use as a store on the loading dock in the left foreground. (CRA Photo Library ref. PEK392)

the demand from passengers on the westbound trains, they were retimed to call at Grange. In the early 1890s an early evening Lakeside to Carnforth train made a slip, as did the Belfast boat train.

From the mid 1890s a pattern emerged, with slips being made from an afternoon and an evening westbound train. At various times one or other would be a boat train from the Midland Railway to Ramsden Dock. In 1910 the afternoon slip was taken off, leaving the evening train, probably with a Midland slip carriage, running until wartime economies forced the Midland to abandon all of its slip workings in December 1916.

Some mention should be made of the occasional trains that appeared from Grange to Morecambe, Lancaster or Carnforth. These usually ran only in the summer months.

During the Great War and afterwards, Vickers shipyard at Barrow obtained labour from a wide area. The FR ran a number of workmen's trains, including ones between Grange and the Island Road station at Barrow. Meanwhile the 'Kendal Tommy' ran only twice a day for the duration of the War and the Bardsea branch service ended altogether in March 1916.

A feature of the Ulverston & Lancaster was excursion trains. These were mentioned in the pages of the Ulverston Advertiser within days of the opening of the line! One of the first brought the employees and their families of Messrs J & W Galloway from Manchester to see the handiwork of their colleagues over the river Leven. The opening of the line also allowed excursions from as far north as Whitehaven to the delights of Manchester (Belle Vue), Liverpool and even exhibitions in London. One of the first was organised by Thomas Cook!

Through the Furness years, tours using scheduled trains and chartered coaches were available to the tourist. These of course developed in the late 1890s with the arrival of Alfred Aslett as FR General Manager, when twenty different tours were available, several utilising sections of the U&LR line.

In the first years of its existence the LMS continued with the general pattern of services introduced by the FR. As well as the services between Carnforth, Barrow and Whitehaven, the odd train ran to Lancaster or Carlisle. In fact for several years the LMS ran a Grange – Lancaster service. Despite the depression, the 1930s saw an expansion of through carriages or through trains from all parts of the LMS system to Lakeside, Barrow and Whitehaven. By the ill-fated summer of 1939, 22 westbound and 20 eastbound trains ran along the U&LR line. Passengers could travel from Manchester, Leeds, Wigan, Liverpool or London for their holidays at destinations along

the old Furness lines. On the Kendal branch, throughout the thirties, many trains started or terminated west of Grange, with some running through to Windermere. Whilst the LMS was enhancing its main-line services, it was well aware of people's preference for buses for local travel, and thus regular passenger trains had been withdrawn on the Lakeside branch in 1938, with a summer-only service provided henceforth.

The 1939-45 war and the period of recovery following saw reduced levels of service, with the Kendal branch services ending from the May 1942 timetable. Again buses were providing the links.

In the post-war years, a summer service was retained on the Lakeside branch, although the intermediate stations were closed to passengers. A novelty on the line, and one of the last acts of the LMS in the area, was the introduction of a sleeping-car service between London Euston and Barrow on 7 October 1947, extended to Workington a few years later. The 1950s saw a return to prosperity, and the train service on the U&LR line was similar to that of 1939, with the added bonus of the sleeping-car service from London. This continued through into the 1960s when the effects of the Beeching report began to take effect and through carriages became a thing of the past. A service of between 11 and 16 trains each way served stations between Carnforth and Barrow, with around 4 each way running through to Carlisle. Since the closure of the main line platforms at Carnforth on 4 May 1970, these have largely run from Preston or Lancaster.

In the 1980s several trains were extended through to Crewe or Liverpool. Other destinations have also been reached for short periods as BR and its successors increasingly sought efficiencies by linking otherwise separate services. The sleeping-car service to London continued until 12 May 1990.

In more recent times services have been split, with services between Barrow and Manchester Airport, stopping only at Ulverston, Grange, Arnside and Carnforth during most of the day interleaved with a Barrow or Millom – Lancaster local service serving all stations.

Privatisation of the railways came to the U&LR line from 7 February 1997. From that date services along the U&LR were included in the North Western trains passenger franchise. Originally a franchise of Great Western Holdings plc, that company was bought out by First Group plc on 30 March 1998. Trains were then run by First North Western. In 2004 the franchises in the north of England were revised resulting in two companies providing trains over the U&LR. Local trains to and from Lancaster are provided by Northern Rail, owned by Serco-NedRailways, whilst Manchester

Cark. On 10 July 1956 ex-FR 0-6-0 No. 52509 pauses from shunting Cark yard whilst ex-LMS Royal Scot 7P 4-6-0 No. 46108 Seaforth Highlander passes with the 1-30 pm Barrow to Crewe passenger train. The loco stands on the site of the sidings of the U&LR Wagon Works whilst the sidings to the left were the original goods yard. (CRA Photo Library ref. PEJ487)

Carnforth F&M Junction. On 13 April 1950 ex-LMS Class 4MT 2-6-4T No. 42428, in early British Railways livery, hauls the 2-05 pm Carnforth to Workington train past Furness & Midland Junction signal box. The rear three vehicles are through carriages off the 6-55 am Euston to Windermere. In the background a Class 5MT 4-6-0 stands at the entrance to the goods yard. The photographer was standing on the site of the Furness & Midland station down platform. *(CRA Photo Library ref. PEV021)*

Airport services, often serving only Ulverston, Grange, Arnside and Carnforth, are provided under the TransPennine Express franchise, operated by a partnership between First Group plc and Keolis.

Since 1974 only Carnforth and Silverdale stations remain in Lancashire, and in recent years the Lancashire County Council have promoted an integration of public transport. They fund the staffed ticket office at Carnforth together with rail-connecting bus services. The Carnforth Connect services started in 2002 and originally ran out to Ackenthwaite, north of Milnthorpe and to Kirkby Lonsdale, although the latter service was later dropped. They also support the Silverdale Shuttle bus link connecting the village with Silverdale station and connecting with most stopping trains. Meanwhile Grange station forecourt remains the focal point for bus services on the Cartmel Peninsular as it has done since the 1920s. Stagecoach, itself an operator of trains elsewhere in the UK and partner in Virgin Trains, now operate the services as direct successors of Grange Motors and one-time LMS subsidiary, Ribble Motor Services.

Goods traffic should not be forgotten – it was, after all, the prime purpose for building the railway. The December 1860 working timetable makes interesting reading, showing two trends: the shipping of ore out of Furness and the importance of handling local goods largely in the opposite direction, on the backs of the trains of empty ore wagons.

Locally, the Ulverstone & Lancaster Railway stations received and despatched goods by three Down trains and one Up. The 12-30 pm Carnforth – Coniston goods was described as 'Thro' & rdsd. Gds. & Lancaster tranships', the 2-40 pm Carnforth to Park as 'Local Goods and Empty Ore Waggons'. The 5-30 pm Carnforth to Barrow Goods was made up of 'Staff. Empties & Local Goods'. The one Up train was the 5-40 am Barrow – Carnforth carrying 'Goods Local & L and Y Ore'. The other Down trains were the 7-40 am Carnforth – Coniston 'Goods & Ore Waggons' and the 6-50 pm Carnforth –to Barrow 'Ore Waggons and Thro' Goods'. As well as the early train already mentioned, eastbound trains largely despatched ore. The 7-50 am Foxfield to Carnforth carried 'Whitehaven Ore', the 1-15 pm Park to Carnforth carried 'Staffordshire Ore' whilst the 2-45 pm Park to Carnforth carried 'Slate and Ore'. The 5-30 pm Barrow to Carnforth ore train was very convoluted as it also served as the 5-30 pm Barrow – Carnforth Passenger as far as Lindal and served as the 7-30 pm Barrow – Carnforth Passenger from Ulverston! The other eastbound train was the 4-30 pm Foxfield to Carnforth 'Through goods' carrying wagons that had left Whitehaven at 1-05 pm.

From the 1870s, stations along the line, together with the quarries, were served by a combination of one or two daily local goods trains, including a roadside van from Carnforth.

For instance in 1877 the U&LR line stations were served by a Carnforth – Coniston goods and coke train and one from Carnforth – Askam, which conveyed the roadside van from Lancaster as well as empty ore wagons and coke. In the opposite direction the stations were served by a Hindpool – Carnforth goods train (including the Midland Roadside Van and Pig Iron). Additionally Cark and Grange local goods were conveyed on a Barrow – Carnforth pig iron train. Meathop and

A Class 40 diesel pulls a Barrow-Crewe train away from Ulverston station in early 1981. At the time the station was undergoing refurbishment. The canopies were in a poor state of repair and were cut back on both platforms, repainted and re-glazed. The view is taken from the steps leading from the former FR terminus and later goods shed. These originally led to the Up platform provided by the Furness for the U&LR. This had been cut back to the short platform, which still exists, when the passenger station was rebuilt in the 1870s, thus allowing staff access between passenger and goods stations. *(Author)*

Carnforth F&M Junction. *On 13 April 1950 ex-LMS Class 4MT 2-6-0 No. M3006 in early British Railways livery hauls a long goods train out of Carnforth F&M Yard bound for Workington. In the background, beyond Furness & Midland Junction Signal Box, an ex-LMS 3F 0-6-0T shunts the goods yard. (CRA Photo Library ref. PEV022a)*

Silverdale. *On 4 August 1955 an unidentified ex-LNWR 0-8-0 hauls a goods train towards Silverdale Level Crossing bound for Carnforth. Note the Up Home signal operated by the ground frame at the crossing. Furness locomotives were driven on the right and some signals had to be positioned on the 'wrong side' to be visible by the drivers. (CRA Photo Library ref. PEJ207)*

Ulverston. *Ex-LMS Class 8F 2-8-0 No. 48703 hauls the 10-15 am Carnforth to Barrow goods train up the grade through Ulverston station on 29 August 1957. The bank engine has still to pass under Princes Street bridge into the station. The line immediately to the left of the loco is the siding used by the Lakeside branch train between turns. The up main line and an up goods loop are beyond. The open wagons are standing in the goods yard, with the goods shed (and former FR passenger terminus) above the train. To the right are the carriage and horse sidings.* (CRA Photo Library ref. PEJ915)

Arnside. *Ex-FR 0-6-0 No. 52509 hauls the 5-05 pm Ulverston to Carnforth goods train through Arnside on 18 July 1956. Note the lighting provided for the walkway from the down platform to the barrow crossing and the station running-in board dating from FR days, with its advice to change for Sandside removed. (CRA Photo Library ref. PEJ515)*

Arnside. *Ex-LMS 4F 0-6-0 No. 44192 hauls the 9-25 am Lindal to Tebay coke empties towards Arnside station on 1 August 1952. It is signalled to run via Sandside to join the Lancaster & Carlisle line at Hincaster Junction and then to Tebay. At Tebay the wagons would be handed over to the North Eastern Region to be taken via Kirkby Stephen to County Durham. (CRA Photo Library ref. PEC843)*

Arnside. *BR Type 2 diesel No. 25157 hauls a down goods train from Carnforth through Arnside on 15 August 1978. (CRA Photo Library ref. PEM217)*

A Class 47 locomotive pulls an empty Merry-go-Round train slowly over the Leven viaduct. These trains took coal from opencast mines in West Cumberland, loaded at Maryport (and for a time Whitehaven), to Fiddlers Ferry power station near Widnes. To the left of the viaduct stands the then-redundant wind-pressure gauge alongside the ruins of what had been at various times a smithy, platelayer's bothy and a signal box. In the background stands Barker Scar and Capeshead from where much of the limestone facing the embankment between here and Cark was quarried. (Alan Johnstone)

Silverdale quarries were served by a daily Meathop - Carnforth stone train, with the empties returning later in the day. Nine years later things were pretty similar with stations served by the Carnforth – Coniston goods (omitting Kents Bank) and Carnforth – Barrow Yard roadside goods. Additionally there was a Carnforth – Arnside and return train specifically to pick up stone from Waterslack quarry. In the Up direction were a Lindal Ore Depot – Carnforth Roadside Goods and a Barrow Yard – Carnforth goods (which also made a detour at Arnside to serve Sandside). Additionally a couple of Fast Goods trains from Barrow to Carnforth stopped at Grange.

Following the Great War and prior to the following depression in trade, local stations were being served by a timetable that would effectively remain until the 1960s, with a goods trains running from Carnforth to Ulverston (serving Grange, Kents Bank and Cark), Carnforth to Sandside (serving Silverdale and Arnside) and Carnforth to North Lonsdale Ironworks.

A feature that appeared even as early as the 1877 timetable was for an Up fast goods train to stop at Cark (and in some years Kents Bank) for fish bound for the markets of industrial Lancashire.

The Lakeside branch saw a daily goods train in each direction right up until closure when it, together with the Bardsea and Canal branches were served by the Carnforth – Ulverston 'trip'.

The line also saw longer distance Fast Goods trains not stopping between Carnforth and Plumpton Junction. A feature of these was that for many years they would stop in either direction to take water at Cark (the last chance before climbing Lindal Bank and, after the diversion of coke empties onto the Hincaster branch in 1916, the last opportunity to take water from a FR water column). 'Fast' may appear a misnomer in these days, since these trains rarely achieved more than 20 mph until well into the 20th century. However the average speed of the roadside goods was even slower!

In 1877, 17 out of the 21 goods trains from Carnforth carried coke, either exclusively or as part of the train. Most was headed for Hindpool and the great Barrow ironworks but trains also served Askam, Ulverston (North Lonsdale, via the steep branch to Ulverston Canal) and Millom (shunted at Lindal Ore Depot). In the opposite direction, of the 23 goods trains, 18 carried pig iron. Two included haematite ore for Wigan. A daily train in each direction carried goods between the Midland Railway and Belfast, via Barrow. Of the four Down goods trains on a Sunday, three conveyed coke (two for Barrow ironworks and one to Lindal) whilst two of the three Barrow – Carnforth goods trains conveyed pig iron and coke empties. The third Up goods train was for Cattle and Perishables, presumably from the Belfast steamer.

Carnforth. BR diesel No. 5706 starts a goods train bound for West Cumberland from the Up Furness line platform circa 1966. These locomotives were concentrated in Cumbria at the time and were often to be seen hauling goods and passenger trains along the U&L. The building to the left of the photograph with the white-painted archway was the office block for the Carnforth Ironworks. The Post Office and Royal Station Hotel can be seen above the station canopies. (M J Borrowdale)

By the 1886 timetable trains could run to and from North Lonsdale via Plumpton. The timetable is less explicit as to which of the 24 Up and 24 Down trains conveyed coke or pig iron. Down Fast Goods trains were running from Carnforth to Barrow (Hindpool or Barrow Yard), Millom, Lindal Ore Depot, Askam Ironworks and North Lonsdale Iron works. Goods on a Sunday were limited to three Fast Goods trains in each direction (one in fact referred to as an Express!). Two of the three Up trains were from Barrow Yard, presumably coke empties and pig iron, and the other from Barrow Docks, with traffic from Ireland. The Down trains were to Barrow Yard, Hindpool and Lindal Ore Depot.

By 1918 the Furness had introduced Traffic Control, as pioneered on the Midland Railway, and could therefore better manage its trains. As already mentioned, wartime economies had made some changes to the traditional methods of working goods trains. Now LNWR locomotives could be seen on the U&LR section and some LNWR trains between points beyond Carnforth and Workington (LNWR) (particularly on a Sunday) were now running via the Furness. Coke trains from County Durham were now running via the Hincaster branch, with both Furness and LNWR locos hauling them between Tebay and the Furness line ironworks (Millom, Askam, Barrow and North Lonsdale). Of the 26 Down trains passing Cark, 8 had LNWR haulage whilst in the opposite direction the LNWR provided power for 7 (plus 1 light engine) of the 29 goods trains. On a Sunday there were four fast goods trains in each direction between Carnforth and Workington (LNWR), each hauled by LNWR locos. The FR used its own locos on the Sunday Fast Goods to and from Barrow Yard.

The hill from Plumpton Junction to Ulverston and Lindal Ore Depot was always a challenge to the westbound goods trains. From 1866, the FR provided bank engines to assist the increasingly heavier trains and avoid a log jam in that section. In the 19th century these were only available from 7-00 am. Any earlier services were allowed to shunt at Plumpton Junction to split their trains and make up to three runs up the bank. Bank engines were available at all hours from the Great War. As mentioned elsewhere, banking by steam locos continued almost to the end of steam on British Rail, since Carnforth shed was one of the last main line steam sheds in Britain. The provision of bank engines for goods trains survived the steam era. Certain freight trains, such as the Northwich to Corkickle soda ash traffic, continued to be assisted from Plumpton Junction into the 1970s.

As with passenger trains, goods and mineral trains continued in LMS and BR days as long as the traffic was there. Thus roadside goods trips ran variously from both Carnforth and Barrow until rationalisation of goods facilities in the early 1960s. As mentioned elsewhere, local goods services were reduced at all except Carnforth, Grange and Ulverston in 1964. Grange continued to be served by a daily Carnforth – Ulverston 'trip' working for another four years after which it ran non-stop to Ulverston well into the 1970s.

Coke trains ran via the Hincaster branch until September 1963 and the closure of Barrow ironworks. The Hincaster branch was closed beyond Sandside , after which Millom's requirements were served via Carnforth until that works also closed. The Sandside to Carnforth stone trains continued until that traffic was lost to the roads. The branch was closed from 31st January 1971. Wagon-load freight (including ammunition and explosives to Barrow and Eskmeals and house coal to Barrow) largely disappeared in the 1970s leaving only the bulk chemical and coal trains. Now the trains of chemicals to the Marchon works at Whitehaven or merry-go-round coal trains from Maryport and Whitehaven are but a memory. Only the occasional nuclear flasks for the Sellafield reprocessing plant and permanent way trains provide a diversion to the otherwise passenger-only Ulverston & Lancaster railway.

A Class 108 Derby Lightweight DMU pulls into Ulverston station with a midday train sometime in the late 1970s. The poor condition of the canopies can be seen: much glass was missing and the ironwork hadn't been repainted since the London Midland Region paint scheme had been applied over 20 years earlier. (Derek Walmsley)

A feature of the U&L line for nearly forty years was the daily train of sodium carbonate to the Marchon detergent works at Whitehaven. No. 40131 pulls the train up the 1 in 82 through Ulverston station on 26 June 1982. (Derek Walmsley)

British Rail Parcels Sector Class 47 approaches Cart Lane crossing, between Kents Bank and Grange, with stock from the Whitehaven-Huddersfield Travelling Post Office in May 1991. The TPO had been a regular feature on the U&L line from 1875 until the last train ran on 28 September that year. Cart Lane grew as a hamlet around one of the points where the Sands road across the Kent Estuary reached the Cartmel Peninsula. Behind the train stands Guide's Farm, home to generations of the Carter family and their successors as Guides to the Kent Sands to the present day. In the background can be seen one of the intermediate block signals that replaced signals controlled from Kents Bank signal box. (Peter Robinson)

Kent Viaduct. A Class 153 unit passes over the viaduct on a winter's morning in 1989. Although the tide is in, there is total calm with neither wind nor waves. The low embankment on the left hand shore beyond the viaduct was built in the mid-1850s to ensure that the River Kent flowed under the viaduct and could not undercut the new railway embankment. The marshes beyond were reclaimed as agricultural land as a result.
(Peter Robinson)

Approaching Grange. From 1991, many longer distance services on the U&L line had been in the hands of Class 156 'Sprinter' DMUs. With the advent of new units under the privatised operators, these were relegated to local services on the route. Here unit 156423, seen here in First North Western livery but branded with the logo of the present operator, Northern Rail, approaches Grange with a Lancaster-bound service on 10 February 2006. The train has just crossed Bailey Lane crossing with its unusual single-storey lodge. Of the buildings in this scene, only the grey building with rounded windows predates the railway and once fronted directly onto the seashore.
(Peter Robinson)

Entering Arnside. The most recent DMUs to see service over the U&L line are First TransPennine Express Class 185 'Pennine' units. A pair of 3-car units enters Arnside station with a Barrow-Manchester Airport train in September 2007.
(Alan Johnstone)

Epilogue:

A Use for Morecambe Bay?

SINCE THE BUILDING of the Ulverstone & Lancaster Railway, the temptation to 'do something' with Morecambe Bay hasn't gone away. Much activity has occurred at different times but, to date, with little effect.

In 1875 there was a scheme to revive land reclamation off Silverdale and Carnforth which had a link to the Ulverstone & Lancaster Railway. Under the title of the Bolton-le-Sands, Warton and Silverdale Reclamation, this was to build an embankment to reclaim land between Arnside Park Point in the north and Hest Bank in the south. The scheme was led by Mr Walduck of Carnforth Ironworks. The engineers were Brunlees & McKerrow. The scheme's original powers to reclaim around 7000 acres, obtained in an Act of 1874, were renewed in 1884. Some work was carried out but had come to a halt by 1879. In 1880 Walduck was even contemplating an embankment right across the Bay, from Hest Bank to a point north of Rampside. He had already negotiated from the Duchy of Lancaster a concession of around 11,000 acres of Cartmel Wharf in the centre of the Bay. With this reclaimed he would raise around a million pounds towards his Hest Bank and Barrow District Railway scheme. This would allow a direct railway from Hest Bank to Barrow. James Brunlees had been approached for his view and had apparently responded favourably. Walduck approached the Duke of Devonshire for his support. Ramsden was ordered to see Walduck, and gathered more information on the scheme for consideration at the FR Board meeting in June 1880. The Duke was duly briefed and declined to give it his support.

Consideration was given to an embankment from Hest Bank towards Barrow during the Second World War, but it wasn't until twenty years later that serious activity took place. In 1964 Manchester Corporation were searching for new sources of water for their growing population and industries. The Ministry of Transport were expanding the growing UK motorway network. The Central Electricity Generating Board was looking for new sites for power stations. A Manchester civil engineer, Leonard Leeming, proposed that a barrage be built from Hest Bank to Bardsea. This could then hold a freshwater lake fed primarily by the rivers Kent and Leven. The 11-mile-long barrage could carry a motorway or dual carriageway and a railway whilst the water could be used both by Manchester Corporation and by the CEGB. A short embankment would link the roads on the barrage with the Cartmel Peninsular off Winder Moor.

Initially support only came from Barrow Borough Council and the Cumberland Development Council. The Ministry of Transport rejected the idea of routing the M6 via the Cumbrian coast. The M6 Lancaster By-pass still ended at Carnforth in the north and the section southwards to join it to the M6 Preston Bypass was still under construction. The Ministry already had plans in place for a route via Tebay and Shap. Manchester Corporation claimed they couldn't justify the scheme on their own. Dr Beeching said it was improbable that the railway would be re-routed, but BR maintained a presence at any meetings. Opposition came almost immediately from the conservationists. The scheme, however, received a high profile, with editorials in the Guardian. Then a General Election occurred with a resultant change of government.

In March 1965 the new Department for Economic Affairs announced a £250,000 study into the Morecambe Bay Barrage. Within months there were rumours of power stations at Flookburgh and Silverdale. By June the Ministry of Land and Natural Resources announced that Sir Alexander Gibb & Partners had been commissioned to cost the study and prepare a programme.

By April 1967 the estimated cost for the Barrage was some £30 million, not including a road. As with the railway schemes of the previous century the proposal was amended to one for two Barrages, from Hest Bank to Humphrey Head and the other across the Leven estuary. Lakes some 16 feet deep would be created. Barrow railwaymen's trade union officials saw a possible road across the Barrage as a bad thing, especially when linked with the Beeching cuts then well underway.

By February 1967 Hydrographic, Aerial and Geophysical surveys were commenced and models built at the Hydraulics Research Station, Wallingford. Readers may recall the drilling rigs across the Bay at that time, associated with the surveys. The study was planned to continue into 1970 with a report to be ready by 1971. The Government were now considering pumped storage reservoirs in the Bay with the possibility of dams further up the Kent and Leven estuaries as well as schemes for the separate barrages and the full barrage. The National Environment Research Council were investigating the environmental issues.

In September 1970 the M6 spur to the A6 and Kendal Bypass were being planned and consideration was made to one of the proposed barrages carrying a link road from Yealand to Lindale on the A590, which would be widened from Levens to Ulverston. In the next month the impact of a barrage on the ports of Barrow, Fleetwood and Heysham was published; silting at Heysham would be a major factor against most of the schemes under consideration although neither Barrow nor Fleetwood would be affected.

A further change of Government occurred with the 1970 General Election. By this time the proposed Arnside Link Road passed through the intended Arnside & Silverdale Area of Outstanding Natural Beauty. A Government enquiry was held at Grange in November and December 1970. The resultant report didn't appear until December 1972. The Department for the Environment rejected the Arnside Link Road in favour of the improvement of dualling the A590 east of the then County Boundary near Meathop and possibly the Lindale Bypass. At the same time the status of Area of Outstanding Natural Beauty was confirmed. Although calls were made to continue with the Barrage scheme they were allowed to fade away after eight years of study and procrastination. Perhaps that had been the Government's plan all along.

To bring this story up to date in terms of using Morecambe Bay, mention must be made of the latest scheme for a 12-mile-long bridge from Heysham to Barrow, incorporating hydro-electric turbines to capture the energy from the tides entering and ebbing from the Bay. The impacts on the environment are but one factor in the scheme this time around. The other is the impact on Barrow and Furness. Will it open the floodgates for investment as Barrow hopes, or will it just make it easier for its residents to find work in 'mainland' Lancashire and what industries remain move away to leave another part of Cumbria as a dormitory for the North West? That, as authors are wont to say, is another story.

Appendix

As the opening of the Ulverstone & Lancaster railway came closer, it had become heavily dependent on the Furness Railway Company for support. Agreement was made between the two companies that the Furness would have responsibility for Signals, Stations and Trains on the U&LR. Consequently early signalling followed contemporary Furness practice.

Each station was controlled from the station office on the time-interval system and using the electric telegraph. At those stations with a passing loop, station signals, with arms for each direction on the same post, were provided together with disc distant signals. These were at Ulverston (north side of cutting, adjacent to the high level station and footbridge), Cark (on the small hill north of the up platform), and Grange (on the down side adjacent to the station level crossing). There were also signals at Carnforth controlled from a signal box. This situation continued after doubling the line, until 1873 and the introduction of block signalling controlled from signal boxes.

Signal boxes on the U&L section of the Furness railway, together with those on the Bardsea branch are tabulated here:

Place	Opened	Closed	Notes
Carnforth	1857	?	*Probably the junction with the L&CR.* Noted in inspection reports, Aug 1857.
Station Junction (1)	30 Jan 1882	23 Oct 1903	**Paley & Austin design, integral to passenger station design -** At end of Furness down platform. Still stands.
Station Junction (2)	24 Oct 1903	Still open	Still stands.
Station Yard		29 Jan 1882	Replaced by Carnforth Station Junction (1) on opening of East curve.
F & M Junction (1)	1867?	1 Mar 1896	**U&L Section -** Old box to Coniston.
F & M Junction (2)	24 Oct 1903	7 Nov 1998	
Silverdale	July 1873	14 Dec 1969	**U&L Section**
Waterslack	6 May 1915	16 Oct 1954	Timber building. No windows to front. Replaced existing ground frame. Block post from opening to approx 6 Oct 1917. *See Ground frames.*
Arnside (1)	July 1873	1876	**U&L Section** ?
Arnside (2)	1876		Date of replacement by current box uncertain. Dates between 1898 and 1910 recorded.
Arnside (3)		Still Open	Still stands. Hincaster branch clipped out of use 10 Sep 1972, removed 8 Oct 1972.
Kent Viaduct (1)	31 May 1885	7 Dec 1885	Temporary box for single line over Kent Viaduct.
Arnside West (2)	9 May 1915	6 Oct 1915	Temporary box for single line over Kent Viaduct.
Meathop	May 1873	4 Aug 1968	**U&L Section -** Meathop Fell at opening (recorded in FR Staff Registers on appointment of first signalman) until before 1877. Opened for daily roadside goods train only c1890 – 26 Mar 1917.
Grange (1)	July 1873	1956	**U&L Section**
Grange (2)	1956	Still Open	**BR LMR**
Kents Bank	July 1873	20 Jun 1942 (or 16 Jul 42)	**U&L Section** - Latterly operated by porter from Cark. SB replaced by IBS and GF (locked from Cark).
Wraysholme	26 Mar 1917	22 Aug 1922	Could be switched out and crossing (with appropriate signals) controlled from pre-existing ground frame.
Cark (1)	July 1873	1952	**U&L Section** - Box remembered as being on soft ground – shook when trains passed.
Cark (2)	1952	18 Jan 1998	**LMS** - Frame and superstructure ex Ulverston Canal.
Ravensbarrow	2 Oct 1883	3 Dec 1932 (8 Jun 1957)	**Single storey -** Conversion of line-side hut. Box closed in 1932 but reopened Whit Mondays (and Aug BH from 1947) for Race traffic to Cark until 1957. Ruins still stand.
Leven Viaduct	2 May 1886	15 Nov 1886	Temporary box (down side, east end of viaduct) for single line working over Leven Viaduct.
Leven East	24 Aug 1913	24 Apr 1915	Temporary box formed from old carriage body (Down side, east end of viaduct) for single line working over Leven Viaduct.

Place	Opened	Closed	Notes
Leven Viaduct	July 1857	Post 1869	**Probably open ground frame** - Signals protecting Sliding Bridge. Mentioned in Inspectors report 1869. Probably open frame
Leven West	24 Aug 1913	24 Apr 1915	Temporary box for single line working over Leven Viaduct. Located in smithy at west end of viaduct.
Leven Junction (1)	By May 1869	17 Mar 1907	
Leven Junction (2)	18 Mar 1907	27 Sep 1952	Last train on branch 7 Aug 1939. Down connection removed April 52. Up connection removed Oct 52.
Plumpton Junction (1)	By March 1869	1882	Also known as Leven Sidings. (1877). (On south side). May predate Lakeside Branch to control sidings.
Plumpton Junction (2)	1882	5 Mar 1898	Signal box (on north side) replacement for opening of Bardsea branch.
Plumpton Junction (3)	6 Mar 1898	19 Mar 2000	Lakeside branch disconnected 8 Mar 1971. Bardsea branch disconnected May 2000 (after demolition).
Ulverston Station (1)	1876	9 July 1898	Accounted for June 1876. Renamed Ulverston East by 23 Apr 1884.
Ulverston East (2)	10 Jul 1898	11 Feb 1934	Replaced by ground frame.
Ulverston (1)	1857?	Before 1882	Assumed name. Originally controlled junction with line to U&LR and goods yard. Ulverston Goods Yard Junction by 3 Feb 1882.
Goods Yard Junction (2)	Before 1882	15 Dec 1900	Renamed Ulverston West by 23 Apr 1884.
Ulverston West (3)	16 Dec 1900	Still Open	Renamed Ulverston 11 Feb 34. Standing.

Bardsea Branch

Place	Opened	Closed	Notes
Ulverston Canal (1)	31 Jul 1882	6 Dec 1931	
Ulverston Canal (2)	7 Dec 1931	1952	**LMS -** Line to North Lonsdale worked as sidings from 27 Mar 33. Superstructure and frame to Cark.
North Lonsdale Crossing	16 Jun 1883	27 Mar 1933/ 20 Aug 38	Probably reopened 1937 when North Lonsdale Ironworks resumed production. Remained as ground frame controlling crossing.
Priory	16 Jun 1883	20 Aug 1938	**Frame in booking office**

Canal Sidings / Paper Mill Sidings — *Marked as SB on 1891 OS Map. Assumed name. May have been ground frame.*

Ground frames:

Place	Location	Controlled	Notes
Carnforth Station	opp Junction Box	Frame Bolt-locked from Signal Box	1915 Appendix (not 1899).
Carnforth F&M Junction	North Siding	Frame Bolt-locked from Signal Box	1915 Appendix.
Waterslack	Waterslack Down Siding *(and Level Crossing)*	Frame not bolt locked from Signal Box	1915 Appendix. First Pointsman Dec 1871. New ground frame opened 2 Oct 1886, replaced 6 May 1915 by signal box. Box used as ground frame 6 Oct 1917 - 16 Oct 1954. Frame replaced and signals removed. Final frame removed and siding closed OOU 14 May 1978.
Arnside	Branch siding	Siding controlled by Tablet	Access to lay-by siding on Hincaster branch.
Grange	Up Sidings	Siding controlled by Key	Access to east end sidings.
Grange	Crossover Road	Frame Bolt-locked from Signal Box	Removed 7 Jul 1940.
Ulverston East			12 Feb 1934 (after closure of East SB) – 22 Sep 1963. Controlled Crossover and exit from Up Goods Loop. Crossover then controlled from Ulverston SB until removed 14 Jan 1973.
Ulverston West	Horse Box Siding	Frame Bolt-locked from Signal Box	
Canal Sidings / Paper Mill Sidings			Marked as SB on 1891 OS Map. Assumed name. May have been ground frame.

Waterslack. This view, looking towards Silverdale, was taken in the 1950s, following the removal of signals. Loaded ballast wagons awaiting collection by the next goods 'trip' in the quarry siding. The siding here appears to have been opened around 1870 but the signal box wasn't erected until 1915, to act as a temporary block post during the rebuilding of the Kent Viaduct. It survived as a ground frame until replaced by a smaller frame nearer points for the quarry siding. (CRA Photo Library ref. PA0025)

Ravensbarrow. Standing alone on the Capeshead Embankment between Cark and the Leven Viaduct stood Ravensbarrow Signal Box. Installed to break the signalling section between Cark and Leven Junction, this box was latterly only opened on Cartmel Race days (August and Whit Bank Holidays) when some special trains from Barrow terminated at Cark. Its original Stevens-pattern signals with spectacles partway up the lattice posts were used until closure. This view was taken on 10 July 1956. (CRA Photo Library ref. PEJ490)

Leven Junction. This late-1930s photograph shows the 1907 signalbox, which replaced the original 1869 box. The Leven Curve runs to the right towards Greenodd Junction and Lakeside. Although the curve was part of the original Lakeside Branch it saw intermittent use. The last train is believed to have passed over the curve on the August Bank Holiday of 1939. (CRA Photo Library ref. PA0060)

Level Crossings:

Miles ex Carnforth	Place	Controlled by	Notes
3m 11ch	Silverdale	Gates Protected by Signals from Ground Frame	Signals after 1899. AHB from 13 Jun 1966
4m 4ch	Waterslack	Gates Protected by Signals from Ground Frame *(not noted in 1915 Appendix)*	Opened circa 1886. Not in 1899 Appendix. Access to Quarry only.
5m 57ch	Black Dyke		Signals added post 1915. AHB from 19 May 1985.
	Arnside		*Between Up and Down platforms* Replaced by Bridge 1874.
	Holme Island		*East of Grange* - Unlisted in Appendices
	Grange Station		Originally at south end of station, moved circa 1862 to north end of platforms. Replaced by subway.
	Bailey Lane		*South of Grange* - Public crossing until 1960s. Unlisted in Appendices.
10m 58ch	Cart Lane		UWB from 3/11/1991.
11m 31ch	Kents Bank	Gates controlled from Signal Box and interlocked with signals.	UWB from 3/11/1991. Interlocking removed with closure of signal box in 1942
12m 42ch	Wraysholme	Gates Protected by Signals from Ground Frame	Signals after 1899. Converted to AOCL 3 July 1981.
	Flookburgh		*East of Cark* - Replaced by Bridge circa 1874.
14m 24ch	Cark		
	Plumpton		*East of Plumpton Junction* - Replaced by Bridge 1875.

Bardsea Branch

Miles ex Plumpton Junction	Place	Controlled by	Notes
0m 46ch	Ulverston Canal	Gates controlled from Signal Box and interlocked with signals	Canal towpath, opposite bank of canal to signal box.
0m 71ch	N Lonsdale Crossing	Gates controlled from Signal Box and interlocked with signals	
1m 58ch	Priory		

Goods and Mineral Train Loads in FR Days:

No train to exceed equal to 55 Vehicles, including Brakes, and special care is to be taken not to overload in stormy weather.

Section	Class	Class A Loco (Ordinary Goods Engines)	Class B Loco (New / Large Goods Engines)
Carnforth – Plumpton Junction	Coal, Coke and Minerals	36	48
	Merchandise	50	54
	Empties	54	54
Plumpton Junction – Lindal Ore Depot	Coal, Coke and Minerals	16	32 (24 in 1915)
	Merchandise	24	36
	Empties	32	48
If Banked	Coal, Coke and Minerals	32	48
	Merchandise	48	54
	Empties	54	54

Gradient Diagrams

Ulverston & Lancaster Railway
Carnforth to Ulverston

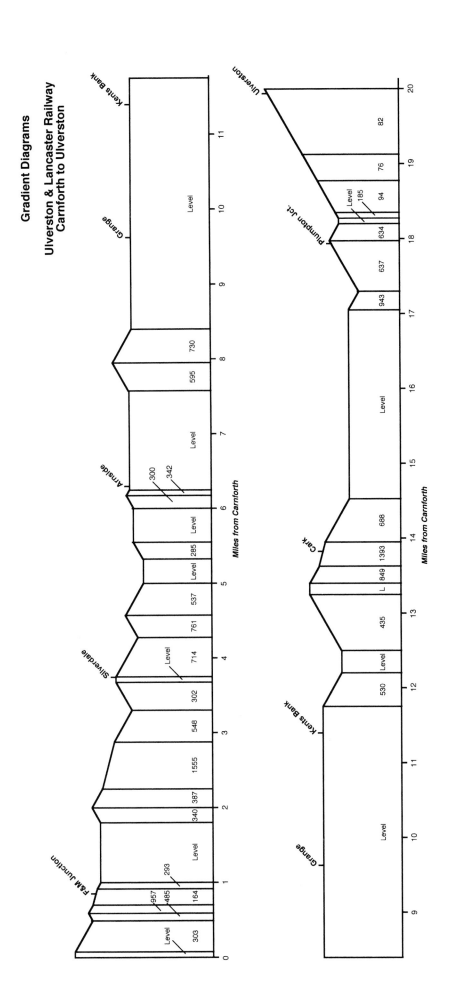

Gradient Diagram
Plumpton Junction - Priory

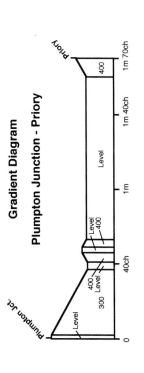

Watering facilities:

Place	Location	Notes
Carnforth	Up Furness Platform	After LMS rebuilding
Carnforth	Down Furness Platform	After LMS rebuilding
Carnforth	Goods Warehouse Siding	Feb 1915 Appendix
Carnforth	FR Engine shed	
Grange	Yard	For Kendal branch train
Cark	Up Main Line	Used by Tebay-bound coke trains after 1916
Cark	Down Main Line (Platform)	Generally used by goods trains before tackling Lindal Bank. Used by coke trains ex-Tebay after 1916
Ulverston	Up platform	Actually opposite east end of up platform
Ulverston	Down Platform	
Ulverston	Yard	

Refuge Sidings (from 1960 Sectional Appendix):

Place	Location	Number of wagons	Notes
Silverdale	Up side	61	
Meathop	Down side	53	
	Up side	33	
Cark	Down	37	
	Down	37	
	Up	53	Behind up side goods yard
Plumpton Junction	Down	93	There had been two refuge sidings here
Ulverston	Up Goods Loop	55	Between Up line and high level goods yard. Removed Sept 1963

Ulverston Canal Signal box circa 1950. *The low fencing beyond the signalbox is on the canal sliding bridge. The canal tow path crosses the railway at the level crossing beyond the bridge. The canal branch left the Bardsea branch just behind the photographer, running behind the signalbox. Following closure, the frame and superstructure of this relatively new box were re-erected at Cark.* *(CRA Photo Library ref. JA0025)*

Acknowledgements

The author would like to thank:

The Archivist and staff at Cumbria Records Office, Barrow;
The National Archive;
The Lancashire Record Office. Preston;

Dr Michael Andrews for his guidance and comments on the text;
Alan Johnstone for the maps, and for leads on the Flookburgh airship factory;
Robert Heywood for information on New Northern Quarries;
Geoff Holme and Ron Herbert for helping resolve several obscure dates;
Peter Holmes for information on the industrial locomotives and railways around Ulverston;
Peter Robinson for assistance with the photographs;
Mike Peascod and the CRA Publications team.

Bibliography

Bradbury, D: *Arnside, a Guide and Community History* (Arnside, 2002)
Gilpin, L R: John Brogden of Manchester (*Cumbrian Railways* Vol. 3 No. 15, 1988)
Gilpin, L R: The Bustling Alexander (*Cumbrian Railways* Vol. 4, No. 6, 1989)
Harris, A: *Carnforth, 1840 – 1900* (Transactions of the Historic Society of Lancashire and Cheshire, Vol. 112, 1961)
Joy, D: *Regional History of the Railways of Great Britain, Vol 14: The Lake Counties* (Newton Abbott 1983)
Layfield, J: *Ulverston Canal & the Construction of Collins Weir* (Ulverston, 2006)
McKeever, R & Layfield, J: *The Industrial Archaeology of South Ulverston* (Ulverston, 2004)
Marshall, J D: *Furness & The Industrial Revolution* (1958, reprinted Beckermet 1981)
Melville, J & Hobbs, J L: *Early Railway History in Furness* (Cumberland & Westmorland Antiquarian & Archaeological Society Tract Series X111, 1951)
Tyler, Ian: *The Gunpowder Mills of Cumbria* (Keswick 2002)

Arnside. Ex-LMS 4F 0-6-0 No. 44387 pilots ex-LMS 5MT 4-6-0 No. 45386 on the 5-43 am Barrow to Carlisle goods train. On 20 May 1955 this train was diverted to run via Sandside and the Lancaster & Carlisle line. *(CRA Photo Library ref. PEJ132)*

Index